Encounter not Perform

After long and distinguished service as an educator, **Frank Wallace, S.J.**, has become active in spiritual direction, the healing ministry, formation and retreat work, Marriage Encounter and charismatic renewal. A native of Australia, he has written for *Review for Religious* and *Human Development*, and is a regular contributor to Jesuit Publications. He resides at the Campion Retreat Centre, Melbourne.

ENCOUNTER not PERFORMANCE

Frank Wallace SJ
on
Prayer

E.J. DWYER

First published 1991 by
E.J. Dwyer (Australia) Pty Ltd
3/32-72 Alice Street
Newtown NSW 2042
Australia
Reprinted September 1991

National Library of Australia
Cataloguing-in-Publication data

Wallace, Frank (Francis James).
Encounter not performance.

Bibliography.
ISBN 0 85574 300 X.

I. Prayer. I. Title.

291.43

Cum permissu Superiorum
Rev. Philip Wallbridge, SJ

Cover designed by Elizabeth Dangrow
Typeset in 10/13 pt Baskerville by Midland Typesetters, Maryborough
Printed and bound in Australia by The Book Printer, Victoria.

Contents

Acknowledgments

The author gratefully acknowledges the use of material from the following works. Every effort has been made to locate the sources of quoted material and to obtain authority for its use.

Your God Is Too Small, J. B. Phillips, Epworth Press, Cambridge, Eng., 1982.

Letters from Westerbork, Etty Hillesun, Grafton Books, London, 1983.

Sadhana, a Way to God, Anthony de Mello, SJ, Gujurat Sahitya Prakash Anand, Gujarat, India, 1982.

'Fragment 73' and 'The Wreck of the Deutschland', *The Poems of Gerard Manley Hopkins*, Oxford University Press, London, 1933.

'The Gentle Water Bird,' *The Poems of Shaw Neilson*, Lothian Books, Port Melbourne, Vic.

Breakaway, Mark Link, SJ, Argus Communications (DLM), Allen, Texas, 1980.

The Collected Works of St John of the Cross, The Collected Works of St Teresa of Avila, Vol 1 and 2, translated by Keiran Kavanaugh and Otilio Rodriguez © 1979, 1976, 1980 respectively by Washington Province of Discalced Carmelites, ICS Publications, 2131 Lincoln Road, N.E., Washington, D.C. 2002.

The Wisdom of A Pauper, Elio Leclerc, Franciscan Publications.

Showings, Julian of Norwich (Classics of Western Spirituality), © 1978, Paulist Press, New York.

The Breath of the Mystic, George A Maloney, SJ, Dimension Books, Denville, New Jersey, 1974.

The Mysticism Debate, Paul Murray, OP, Franciscan Herald Press, Chicago, 1977.

Christian Mysticism, Harvey D Egan, SJ, Pueblo Publishing, New York, 1984. Used with permission.

Scivias (Know The Ways), translated by Bruce Hozeski, © 1985 by Bear and Company, Inc., from *Hildegard of Bingen's Book Of Divine Works (with letter and songs)*, edited by Matthew Fox, OP, © 1987 by Bear and Company, Inc; and from *Meditations with Hildegard of Bingen*, adaptations by Gabriele Uhlein, © 1983 by Bear and Company, Inc.; permission to excerpt has been granted by the publisher, Bear and Company, PO Drawer 2860, Santa Fe, NM 87504-2860.

The Cloud of Unknowing and *The Book of Privy Counselling*, Image Books, Doubleday, New York, 1973.

A Pilgrim's Journey: The Autobiography of Ignatius Loyola, translated with notes by Joseph N Tylenda, SJ, Michael Glazier, Wilmington, Delaware, 1985. Used with permission of The Liturgical Press, Collegeville Minnesota.

Spiritual Letters, Dom John Chapman, The New Ark Library, Sheed and Ward, London, 1959.

Francis de Sales, Michael de la Bedoyere, Harper and Brothers, New York, 1960.

Introduction to the Devout Life, St. Francis de Sales, trans. Monsignor Ryan, Longman, Green and Company, London, 1953.

Treatise on the Love of God, trans. Rev John K Ryan, 2 vols., Tan Books, Rockford, Illinois, 1975.

The Joy of Full Surrender, Jean-Pierre de Caussade, edited by Hal M. Helms, © 1986, Paraclete Press, Orleans, MA 02653. Used by permission.

Spiritual Letters, Jean-Pierre de Caussade, 2 vols., translated by Algar Thorold, Burns Oates and Washbourne Ltd., London, 1948.

Resource material on Mary MacKillop published by the Archives of The Sisters of St. Joseph, North Sydney.

The Seven Mountains of Thomas Merton, Michael Mott, Sheldon Press, London, 1984. Used with permission of SPCK, London.

Excerpt from *Murder in the Cathedral* by T S Eliot, Faber and Faber Ltd., London; copyright 1935 by Harcourt Bruce Jovanovich, Inc. and renewed in 1963 by T S Eliot, reprinted by permission of the publisher.

Scripture texts are taken from *The Jerusalem Bible*, published and copyright 1966, 1967 and 1968 by Darton Longman and Todd Ltd. and Doubleday and Co. Inc. and used by permission of the publishers.

Foreword

What, another book on prayer? I know of many fine books on the subject, yet I still want to write this one. Perhaps it is something like the way artists have kept on painting Madonnas. Fra Angelico's *Annunciation* didn't say everything about Mary; others felt impelled to express her mystery, and so we have many wonderful tributes, none of which exhausts the theme.

Through the ages there have been many writers on prayer, and we have been helped by them. I look at some of them, and their work, in this book. And that is a good reason for writing.

Today there is a hunger for prayer within and without the Churches. More and more people are making pilgrimages within, to their own hearts, impelled by the Spirit of God, and discovering 'the Spirit who raised Jesus from the dead living within'.

I have been privileged to journey with many of these pilgrims of the heart, and I welcome this opportunity to say 'Thank you' to them, and to Anthony de Mello, whose workshops, books and friendship enriched me. Just as the stories of these people have helped me, my story may help others to see how God calls us.

For twenty-seven years I was engaged in teaching and administration, first of all at St Ignatius' College, Riverview, Sydney, then at Xavier College, Kew, Melbourne, and finally at St Ignatius', Norwood and Athelstone, Adelaide. Teaching I enjoyed, administration I did as best I could. They were rewarding and happy years and I expected to see out my life in this important ministry of education.

My journey, however, took a very different turn when at the end of a heavy building programme in Adelaide I was given a sabbatical. I felt as though a weighty load had been lifted from my shoulders. The building programme, the fund raising campaigns, the financial burdens, the turbulence of the 1960s , the negative attitude toward authority figures and the winds of change had cost me more than I had been prepared to admit.

A number of different experiences during that sabbatical helped free me. Chaplaincy in a hospital in New York, working in a parish in San Jose, experiencing Marriage Encounter and the Charismatic Renewal—all these helped me see new doors opening.

When I returned to Australia I was no longer appointed to schools. Instead I was assistant to the Provincial. This enabled me to help establish Marriage Encounter in Australia, and to join in the Charismatic Renewal, to work with Mary Rogers in the Healing Ministry. Later I was placed in charge of Tertianship, the programme Jesuits follow after ordination. It was all so different from work in the schools.

Somebody once sent me a card that read: 'Thank God I am no longer an oak tree. I am a willow: I can bend'. This, I believe, was the freedom to which I was being led. For me, being an oak tree had been the only way to face the challenges presented. Becoming a willow released gifts that had been hidden by the masks I had found it necessary to wear. Moving into inner freedom is a grace-filled journey. Perhaps my story will help others to travel that way.

The many Marriage Encounter couples I met opened me up to a wonderful world of feelings, communication and relationships. The Jesuits in the Tertianship programmes I had charge of, and the many retreatants in directed retreats and in group retreats, enlightened me about the varied ways of the Lord and encouraged me. The Charismatic Renewal freed me from many tensions (tension is the greatest enemy to prayer, said Tony de Mello), the retreats and ministry with the Uniting Church widened my vision. Mary Rogers led me into the Healing Ministry and the groups I have prayed with for healing, especially the Richmond group in Victoria to which Father Frank Maher SJ and I belong, teach me something of compassion and of weakness that is strength.

Finally, having explored something of the richness of Western spirituality, I thought it would be exciting to provide a brief introduction that would, I hoped, encourage others to read some of our Christian classics.

So I dedicate this book to all those wonderful people who have been instruments of the Lord's healing, and who have taught me that prayer is an encounter, 'a surprise discovery', not a performance.

PART I

Introduction

There are two parts to this book. In Part I I explore what prayer is. By considering different aspects of it, clearing up misunderstandings, and exploring the growth many experience as they move from vocal prayer to meditation, to contemplation and to simple ways of praying, I hope I will make it clear that all genuine prayer is an encounter.

At the end of each chapter I provide topics for reflection and discussion. These aim at summing up the matter presented. In particular I have in mind their use in prayer groups such as the ones I have worked with over the years.

Such sharing taught me much about the variety of the Spirit's gifts in prayer, and deepened my understanding of prayer as an encounter with a passionate God. This brings us to the threshold of mysticism.

Part II presents just a few memorable mystics who help us all by their teaching and their example. By giving brief introductions to the lives and works of these men and women, I seek to uncover something of the rich treasures of Western mysticism and to encourage the reading of these classics. After all, if we are called to be mystics, as Rahner claims, a clear understanding of mysticism is needed.

I have provided a reading list in the hope that this brief, popular presentation will stimulate deeper reading.

1.

Prayer— An Encounter, Not a Performance

Some time back I was giving a session on prayer to parishioners of the Uniting Church in Balwyn, Victoria. On the wall was a banner bearing these words:

L is Listening
L is Learning
L is Loving
L is Living

This is what I understand prayer to be. As I reflect upon the four L's, I see even more clearly that my first Marriage Encounter weekend sixteen years ago, and all those since, have been telling me the same story of the four L's. Prayer is an encounter, not a performance.

The lifeblood of any relationship is communication. When I stop communicating, the friendship withers and dies. If my communication is superficial, if my friend and I talk only about trivia, then the friendship will be shallow. The deeper the communication, the greater the intimacy.

The lifeblood of the communication is listening. As I listen to what my friend is communicating, verbally and non-verbally, I lose myself in my friend, I let go of my agenda. I encounter him or her.

The lifeblood of the listening is responding. My friend needs to know that he or she is being heard. How often I feel down when I think I am not heard! By responding I accept my friend and he or she encounters me.

What is true of human relationships is true also of our relationships with God. Communication between God and me, listening to each other, responding to each other, all nourish our relationship. So prayer is communicating, listening, responding, nourishing. It is a *mutual* encounter.

There is, however, a risk of being so concerned with all this that I am continually watching how well I am doing. When that happens all I meet is myself, or rather my activity, and not God. My prayer has become a performance and is not an encounter. There is a story of the young man talking to the girl. He has been talking at some length and suddenly he stops. 'Sorry, Jean,' he says, 'I'm talking all the time about me. Let's talk about you. What do you think of me?' A good parallel with some of my praying, I confess.

When my prayer is a performance I occupy centre stage. I do all the talking and the thinking. As Armand Nigro comments, my prayer gets 'jammed up' with all my activity. Preoccupation with my needs, my sins, my apostolate, my friends, my prayer, my achievements and my failures makes for a one-sided relationship. God is unable to get through to me. When I slow down and listen, God can be heard. A monologue is not the right tool for building a relationship because it involves no true communication, no listening. There is no prayer unless God is met. When we meet God and God meets us, we are present to each other. In a monologue there is no mutual presence, no giving and receiving.

And prayer is giving and receiving. An encounter is a meeting in some depth between two people. There is self-revelation and open trust. It is an experience of intimacy as you tell me who you are and I tell you who I am. This personal exchange can grow deeper and deeper as our communication is more trusting. If I tell you what I do, where I work, where I live, where I come from, you learn much *about* me. You may just meet the masks I wear, not me. When I tell you of my hopes, fears, joys, failures, weaknesses and feelings, you may come to know me. Knowledge *about* does not create a loving relationship. For this, knowledge *of* the other is needed.

I recall a woman telling me that she had been married twenty years and her husband still didn't know her. Then she surprised me as she said, 'I never told him who I was'. Another said that for her husband sex was intimacy, whereas for her it was 'just the icing on the cake'. 'If only he would tell me what goes on inside him!' she cried. She was longing for a true encounter, not a performance.

Both marriages would have been enriched if there had been deeper communication. Often on a Marriage Encounter Weekend I have seen a marriage revitalised when one or both have experienced being loved for *who* they are, not for *what* they do. A quotation on my Marriage Encounter Calendar tells me: 'Love is revealing myself. We are as healthy and whole as we are open and honest with ourselves and others'.

The same holds, I believe, in our relationship with God. When prayer is a real encounter with God we take off our masks, we stand naked before him, we experience being loved for who we are. In turn we, through his gift, experience who he *is* rather than what he *does*. Often our relationship with God suffers because all we are concerned about is what he is doing or not doing. We fail to search for who he is.

If, however, my prayer is a performance, the focus is on *doing*, winning approval, achieving, and not on *being*, not on the relationship, the intimacy of shared lives. I am so busy performing that I don't let God tell me who he is, that he loves me as I am, accepts me as I am. It does not occur to me to let him thank me for giving my life to him, for listening to one of his brothers and sisters, for helping another of his children. Slowing down to listen means I can allow God to tell me he loves me. 'Be still and know that I am God.' It helps me learn that I am not God, I am not the major partner. What God does in prayer is always more important than what I do. The trap of a spirituality based on trying harder is that it exaggerates the human as it neglects the divine activity.

In performance prayer there is very little listening, yet listening is the lifeblood of communication. When I see prayer as a performance, I am led into comparisons. I measure my actual self with the ideal self, to borrow the helpful insights of Karen Horney. Seeing how far I fall short of the ideal pray-er, I become discouraged and begin to die. The self-talk of 'I should do this', 'I ought to be able to do better', is destructive. Seeing prayer as a performance keeps me under the tyranny of the *should*, the *ought*, and perfectionism lands me with much guilt. All I have then is harmful introspection and a bad case of narcissism, as I compare the actual self and the ideal self. This is not prayer at all, because God has not come into the picture.

When prayer is an encounter, the effects are very different. There is honest revelation, as I come before God just as I am, angry, tired, disappointed, sad, happy, grateful. No pretending to be other than I am. This is authentic, without any comparisons or masks. And I relate to God as well as I can and I allow God to be God. I know this is not easy, but in a true encounter with God or anybody else, the condition is one of freedom and trust. Authentic prayer just happens when I am truly myself and God is truly God and we meet in some depth. This is an encounter.

Father Gabriel Calvo, a Spanish priest, designed the programme Encuentre Conjugal (Marriage Encounter). The Spanish word '*encuentre*', says Calvo, means 'surprise discovery'. He later developed 'Marriage Retorno' to help couples with their prayer.

Just as an encounter with a friend whom I trust is life-giving and nourishing for our relationship, so too is the encounter with God. When I leave prayer discouraged and feeling guilty, I need to reflect on the nature of the prayer. Was it an encounter or a performance?

In any performance I tend to be conscious of what I am doing, whether I am pleasing the other, and what the other is doing, or thinks of me. So I don't meet the other, I only see his or her actions. When there is an encounter, I meet the person. Apply this to prayer and the same is true. When my prayer is a performance, I am concerned about what I am doing and perhaps also with what God is doing. So performance prayer tends to involve a destructive image of God.

When I am feeling down or low in self esteem, my prayer is more likely to be performance. I am afraid to risk the self-revelation of an encounter and so I will try to win love by doing good to others, like the lady in *The Screwtape Letters* 'who went about doing good to others: you could tell the others by their hunted looks!' Encounter prayer meets the God who loves unconditionally and gratuitously.

Encounter prayer is all about being and loving, rather than about doing. Encounter prayer is 'surprise discovery'.

Reflections

1. Reflect slowly, one by one, on the following descriptions of prayer. Which one fits your experience? Which one would appeal to you?

   Choose the one that most appeals to you and then imagine Jesus telling you that the description you chose is what prayer is. Tell him of your thoughts and feelings.

'Prayer is not much thinking, but much loving' (St Teresa of Jesus).

Prayer is an encounter, not a performance.

Prayer is reaching for the real, not the idealised; the real God, not the idealised God; the real, true self, not the false, idealised self.

Prayer is wrestling with God.

Prayer is being present to oneself, and to God.

'Prayer is an elevation of the soul to God, to adore him, to bless his holy name, to praise his bounty and mercy, to return him thanks for his benefits, and to ask him for all necessaries for soul and body.' (Catechism 1934).

Prayer is a journey inwards that unlocks the keys of the heart.

Prayer is Listening, Learning, Loving, Living, Nourishing.

Prayer is the Spirit of Jesus breathing within me.

2. Write a letter to Jesus about your prayer life: when you pray, why you pray, how you pray. Be honest and describe it as it is, not as you think he would like it to be.

3. Imagine Jesus reading your letter carefully. Then he answers it. In imagination become Jesus and write the response he makes to you.

4. Tom says: 'Sometimes I worry that when I am praying I am really just talking to myself'. How would you respond?

5. Who am I? Write out a brief description of yourself, putting down whatever comes to mind, without much deliberation. Now reflect on your answer. Does it describe what you do or who you are? Is it mostly negative or positive? Using 'feeling' words leads to a deeper revelation, for example, 'I am often sad', 'I am usually happy'.

Reading List

Anthony de Mello SJ *Sadhana, A Way to God.* Gujarat Sahitya Prakash Anand, Gujarat, India, 1978.

Anthony de Mello SJ *Wellsprings.* Gujarat Sahitya Prakash Anand, India, 1984.

Karen Horney MD *Our Inner Conflicts.* W.W. Norton & Company Inc. New York, 1966.

Karen Horney MD *Neurosis and Human Growth.* W.W. Norton & Company, New York, 1970.

2.

Second-hand Gods for Sale

Why and how I communicate with another will be influenced by my relationship with that other. If I see him or her as an enemy, and I am afraid and feel threatened, my communication will be cautious, restricted and lack spontaneity. I will be afraid to speak freely. If the person is a powerful authority figure who is able to reward me, punish me or control some aspect of my life, again I may be very reserved when I am communicating. If he or she is, however, a friend whom I trust, somebody I like and who I know likes me, there will be greater freedom and spontaneity in our communication. This is true of all relationships, including the relationship I have with God. It is important, therefore, to know how I see God if I am to be helped in my life of prayer.

Some time ago, I was talking to a woman who told me she would like to have a baby, but she added, 'I am afraid because I have led such a wicked life that I am sure God will punish me and the baby will be deformed or even stillborn'. That is a frightening image of God, and yet that was how she saw God! He was a punishing God and she was afraid of him, though she said that he was just and she thought she deserved whatever he did to her.

I still remember vividly a time when as a very little boy I was terrified that I would commit a mortal sin, and as I was running across to get to Confession I would be knocked over and killed and go to Hell for all eternity. My God was very just, but surely not a God who loved me, or that I saw as loving me. He really was a 'gotcha' God. Fortunately, I no longer see that kind of God.

I meet people whose images of God are so destructive that I can't help thinking it would be better for them to be atheists than to be meeting the destructive God who has become part of their lives. There is one woman with deep psychological problems who thinks that she will be cured by multiplying her prayers, reading scripture, and visiting the Church. But all of that makes things worse, because she is forever meeting a God who complains and who punishes, and who is unrelentingly stern. When I say to her 'Pray less, read the scriptures less often,' she finds it very hard to accept that advice, because of her fear. She is trapped by her concept of God.

Destructive Images of God

J. B. Phillips, many years ago, wrote *Your God is Too Small,* in which he discussed some destructive images of God, for example, the resident policeman, parental hangover, managing director, second-hand God and so on. All of these images of God, he concluded, are destructive because they prevent us from glimpsing who God really is, and inhibit healthy growth.[1]

The second-hand God is the God that somebody else—school, Church, parents—has passed on to you. If it is never assimilated, if that God is never really met in your own heart, it will never be your God, but somebody else's God. Your prayer to such a God would tend to be routine and have very little heart in it. It is a performance, rather than an encounter.

If your God is the great examiner in the sky, and life is a test that you will either pass or fail—and that is how I have heard some describe life—then in your prayer you will always be trying to please that examiner and pass the exam, and when you see failures you will be discouraged.

The fix-it God is another image that can take hold of us: the God we always run to, expecting him to solve everything with his magic wand, while we sit back and do nothing. Such a God never allows us to become mature, to grow, to make our own adult decisions.

Then there is the God of calamities. When anything bad happens to me, I say it's the will of God. That is a way of avoiding responsibility for my own life. Alas, it carefully conceals the God of love from me.

The policeman, judge, Father Christmas, the Ombudsman in the sky, and so on, are other images that are held of God.

Prayer to such Gods becomes a way of pleasing and placating, a way of avoiding responsibility, a way of remaining infantile. They all have in common this, that the love of God is conditioned by how I behave and perform. No wonder, then, that my prayer is a performance, not an encounter, because I don't want to get too close to that kind of God. There can be no growth in intimacy with a destructive image of God.

God of the Hundred Per Cent

For good people, as J. B. Phillips says, and my own experience confirms, the commonest and most destructive image of God is the God of the hundred per cent. This is another name for perfectionism. This God is never satisfied with me unless I perform perfectly. I pray because I ought to, out of a sense of duty, not because I want to. I come away from prayer disappointed, feeling guilty. Why? Because I am not perfect. The God of the hundred per cent loves me conditionally and keeps me under 'the tyranny of the should'.[2]

The danger of this image of God is that it masquerades as something that is good. It is built up from distortions of teachings about a God who wants us to come to *wholeness*. Misunderstandings of the teachings of the Church, of scripture and of parents can twist this ideal of wholeness into the impossible aim of being *perfect*.

Now, only God is perfect. If I think I am perfect, I have renounced my state of being a creature. If I am perfect, I have no need of Jesus, for his ministry is precisely a ministry of healing our imperfections. The God of the hundred per cent is definitely the God who loves me *conditionally*. His love grows and diminishes according to the way I perform. Since I can never be flawless, I must come out of prayer feeling guilty and discouraged because I have let down my God of the hundred per cent.

The conflict that Jesus had with the Pharisees and the leaders in Jerusalem was about their image of God. For them, true religion consisted in the perfect observance of the law. In practice, this meant that the love of people was subordinate to this external perfect observance, hence they were horrified that Jesus should heal on the Sabbath Day. The God of Jesus however, was never the God of the hundred per cent. He was always the God of love. All through his ministry he was trying to reveal that God is love.

The story of the crazy farmer, as Andrew Greeley describes him, who gave the same pay to all the workers even though they worked different hours, is not about a God of the one hundred per cent; that same remarkable, forgiving father loved equally the younger and the older son in the story of the prodigal son; God our Father loved us so much that he sent his son to live on earth. All these instances are revealing to us the God who loves us *unconditionally*. A false God is easily recognisable. He or she loves *conditionally*. The true God that scripture and Jesus reveal loves us unconditionally and gratuitously.

It is necessary for the healthy development of my prayer life that I discover whether the God I am relating to loves me unconditionally. A distinction between the notional assent I give to God and the real assent, following Cardinal Newman, can be helpful.

The notional idea of God is the image of God that I hold in my head, and that has gone no deeper: I say and think God loves me because I was told so. But the truth has never been appropriated by me, and I have very little experience or inner conviction of a loving God. I have never made this image of God my own.

The real assent is the surrender not only of the mind but of the whole person. The image of God involved here is *operational*, that is, it deeply influences my behaviour and my feelings, as well as my thinking. By listening to my feelings and noting my behaviour, I can discover whether or not I am relating to the God who loves me unconditionally.

The lady afraid to have a baby operates from the idea of a punishing God, whatever she might think or say about God loving her. When I find I am operating *only* out of a sense of duty, because I ought to, or should do something, or when I leave my prayer guilty and discouraged, I need to discern what image of God is influencing me. When I miss a meal, I feel hungry, not guilty. When I miss my prayer, do I feel hungry or guilty? The answer may tell me something about my real image of God.

Hannah Hurnard, in her delightful book *The Hearing Heart*, says that at one stage in her life she could not pray to Jesus. She could pray to the Father and to the Spirit, to God, but not to Jesus. Why was this so? She tells us that every time she thought of Jesus, she thought of that saying 'If you wish to be my disciple, you must take up your cross daily and come follow me', and that frightened her. She was scared that if she got close to Jesus, she would suffer in some way or other, that it was a condition of being close to him to be miserable and to suffer.

You can see there how her operational concept of Jesus was really a distorted one. There is much more to Jesus and being close to him than suffering, just as there is much more to love than pain, even though pain may be part of love. Hannah Hurnard describes how she was freed from her distorted image of Jesus, so that she was able to pray to him as well as to the Father and the Spirit.[3]

Etty Hillesum was a remarkable Dutch Jewish woman who died at Auschwitz. Her diary and her letters from Westerbork, smuggled out of the camp and published in 1983, contain an inspiring story of her relationship with God. In the letter she wrote on 18 August 1943, just a few months before her death, she described beautifully who God was for her.

> You have made me so rich, O God, please let me share out your beauty with open hands. My life has become an uninterrupted dialogue with you, O God, one great dialogue. Sometimes when I stand in some corner of the camp, my feet planted on your earth, my eyes raised towards your heaven, tears run down my face. Tears of deep emotion and gratitude.

When we remember all the sufferings she was enduring, the persecution before and during her imprisonment in the camp, we can only marvel that she could find there a God of love.[4]

It is important that we allow God to reveal himself to us, and for that we need to slow down, as Psalm 46 says, and 'Be still and know that I am God'.[5] I had been praying on Psalm 46 when I came to realise that the God revealed to me there is not the God of power who comes with a magic wand and changes situations. The God revealed is the God ever present in time of trouble. It seemed to me that there was a big difference between praying to a God of power and praying to the God of presence.

When we pray to the God of power, often we are asking God to change the situations we are in, and that is certainly right. Jesus did that in the Agony in the Garden. He asked the Father to take the chalice away, to change the situation. The incredible thing was that the Father did *not* take the chalice away, but came and stood with Jesus to strengthen him so that he could move through the Passion to the Resurrection. God did not change the situation, but changed Jesus' attitude.

In the weekly healing group to which I belong, I have come to see more clearly that the God who wants to support me is more consoling than the God who changes the situation. The members of that group have taught me that God is more interested in people than in situations.

A day I once spent with Compassionate Friends was a powerful experience of a God ever present in time of trouble, a God who, by standing with people in their situation, deepened their faith, their hope, their love, their courage. Certainly, on that day we were not meeting the God who comes with a magic wand to change situations; we were meeting a God who helped us to find strength in the situation. We were meeting the God who met Jesus in the garden. We were being schooled in compassion, which is shared helplessness.

Emma Pierce, in her book *Passion for the Possible,* says that each person has the power to heal himself or herself, but that the support of friends and God is needed.[6] Meeting the God ever present in time of trouble helps us to become aware of our own inner strength, enables our hidden self to grow strong. But when I pray to the God of the magic wand, I run the risk of remaining infantile.

These experiences with the people who have met the God ever present in time of trouble have opened up to me further revelations of who God is. I have seen the danger of just seeing what God does, or does not do, and being blinded to who God is.

The 'encounter with self talk' in a Marriage Encounter Weekend helped me to get behind the masks that can conceal the hidden self, masks which can prevent people from knowing me. What I noted about the masks was that they were concerned with what I was doing. When I just meet what God does, I can be caught up in blaming him. It's like a little child who can only see or hear the parents' punishment. Seeing what they do, the child cannot see the love that is prompting the punishing, the person behind the deeds. When I can look beyond what God does or does not do, I look behind the mask and I discover who God is. Again, it is Psalm 46 that helps me in that understanding. It also frees me from the great risk of trying to play God in my life or in the lives of others. A true encounter always takes place in a condition of freedom that allows both to be who they are. Psalm 46 has helped me to let God be God, and when that happens I can let myself be who I am.

In my work with groups I have seen the power of fantasy exercises in revealing people's images of God, and what their relationships with those Gods are. I take the exercise from Tony de Mello's book *Sadhana,* or the exercise from Marlene Halpin's *Imagine That* called 'the God tree'. De Mello's fantasy suggests searching for God and forming a symbol of God. Halpin's suggests imagining God as a tree and by further use of imagination exploring one's relationships.[7]

The strength of fantasy work is that it takes people out of their heads and permits them a freedom of imagination that can break open their deepest emotions and feelings. It also has in it the power to heal and strengthen. In the sharings that have followed these fantasy exercises, there is a spontaneity and a deeper insight, through symbolism, into people's relationship with their God. I also find that people in the group, for the most part, talk freely and happily about the experience. Normally there is much more laughter at this time than there was when they were talking about their prayers. The relationship to God in the mind can be much more restrictive than the relationship to God in the imagination. When we are able to integrate both, I think God is revealing Himself to us in a true way.

The only way I ever get to know anybody is by spending time in that person's company and by being prepared to reveal myself to that person and to listen to the revelations the person makes to me. Ultimately, only God can reveal to you who he is. Anything else—books, courses, scripture, Church, other people—gives you second-hand knowledge.

Gerard Manley Hopkins writes (in 'Fragment 73'):

> Thee, God, I come from, to thee go,
> All day long I like fountain flow
> From thy hand out, swayed about
> Mote-like in thy mighty glow.[8]

In another poem, 'The Wreck of the Deutschland', he writes:

> Thou mastering me
> God! giver of breath and bread;
> World's strand, sway of the sea;
> Lord of living and dead;
> Thou hast bound bones and veins in me, fastened me flesh,
> And after it almost unmade, what with dread,
> Thy doing; and dost thou touch me afresh?
> Over again I feel thy finger and find thee.[9]

It seems to me that in those two poems Hopkins is presenting different images of God. In the first one, God seems to be a gentle God, one who is very welcoming. In the second, the God presented is powerful, somewhat awesome and also very intimate. I wonder which image most appeals to you. Both, of course, are valid.

Reflections

1. Read Mark 3, the story of Jesus curing the man with a withered hand. How would you describe the operational God of the Pharisees?

2. Listen to the tape 'His Greatest Delight', sung by Paul Gurr (*Whispers,* Kevin Bates SM, A.C.A.V.C., Homebush, NSW, Australia). What is the image of God that is presented? Have you ever considered that God is like that? Do you meet a happy, laughing God in your prayer, at Mass?

3. How free are you in expressing your anger towards God? What does your answer tell you about your God?

4. Think of a symbol (e.g. flame, wind, rock, maternal love . . .) that best expresses for you who your God is. What are the qualities in it that appeal to you?

5. In your prayer are you talking *for* God, *to* God or *with* God? What might this tell you of your image of God?

6. A man is very sick. He tells you that God has sent him the sickness to try him. What do you think is his operational image of God? Do you like his God?

7. Look back over your life to see how your image of God has influenced your decisions.

8. Whom do you pray to—Father, Jesus, Spirit, Mother, God, Trinity? Why?

9. The Catechism I used at school read

   Q. Who is God?
   A. God is the Creator of heaven and earth and of all things and the Supreme Lord of all.

Q. How many Gods are there?
A. There is but one God, who will reward the good and punish the wicked.

What do you think of these images of God?

10. Read chapter 17 of John's Gospel. What do you think is Jesus' operational image of God?

11. The following poem by John Shaw Neilson 'The Gentle Water Bird' describes how he changed from seeing a God who terrified him to appreciating a God who loves him. How was he helped in this growth? Can you think of a similar growth in your own relationship with God?

The Gentle Water Bird[10]

(for Mary Gilmore)

In the far days, when every day was long,
Fear was upon me and the fear was strong,
Ere I had learned the recompense of song.

In the dim days I trembled, for I knew
God was above me, always frowning through,
And God was terrible and thunder-blue.

Creeds the discoloured awed my opening mind,
Perils, perplexities—what could I find?
All the old terror waiting on mankind.

Even the gentle flowers of white and cream,
The rainbow with its treasury of dream,
Trembled because of God's ungracious scheme.

And in the night the many stars would say
Dark things unaltered in the light of day:
Fear was upon me even in my play.

There was a lake I loved in gentle rain:
One day there fell a bird, a courtly crane:
Wisely he walked, as one who knows of pain.

Gracious he was and lofty as a king:
Silent he was, and yet he seemed to sing
Always of little children and the Spring.

God? Did he know him? It was far he flew . . .
God was not terrible and thunder-blue:
—It was a gentle water bird I knew.

Pity was in him for the weak and strong,
All who have suffered when days were long,
And he was deep and gentle as a song.

As a calm soldier in a cloak of grey
He did commune with me for many a day
Till the dark fear was lifted away.

Sober-apparelled, yet he caught the glow:
Always of Heaven would he speak, and low,
And he did tell me where the wishes go.

Kinsfolk of his it was who long before
Came from the mist (He surely willed it so)
Bearing great happiness to all below?

Long have I learned that all his speech was true;
I cannot reason it—how far he flew—
God is not terrible nor thunder-blue.

Sometimes, when watching in the white sunshine,
Someone approaches—I can half define
All the calm beauty of that friend of mine.

Nothing of hatred will about him cling:
Silent—how silent—but his heart will sing
Always of little children and the Spring.

John Shaw Neilson

Notes

1. J. B. Phillips, *Your God is Too Small,* Epworth Press, London, 1982.
2. Karen Horney MD, *Neurosis and Human Growth,* W. W. Norton & Company, New York, 1970, pp. 64–85.
3. Hannah Hurnard, *The Hearing Heart,* Olive Press, London, 1975.
4. Etty Hillesum, *A Diary 1941–43,* Triad Panther Books, London, 1983; *Letters from Westerbork,* Grafton Books, 1988, p. 116.
5. Psalm 46. The scripture texts throughout the book are taken from the *Jerusalem Bible,* Darton, Longman & Todd, London, 1966.
6. Emma Pierce, *Passion For the Possible,* P. G. Pierce, Gladesville, NSW.
7. Anthony de Mello SJ, *Sadhana, a Way to God,* Gujarat Sahitya Prakash Anand, Gujarat, India, 1978, p. 79; Marlene Halpin, *Imagine That,* W. C. Brown Company, Dubuque, Iowa, 1982, pp. 63–8.
8. Gerard Manley Hopkins, 'Fragment 73', *The Poems of Gerard Manley Hopkins,* ed. Robert Bridges, 2nd edition, Oxford University Press, London, 1933, p. 91.
9. Gerard Manley Hopkins, 'The Wreck of the Deutschland', *The Poems of Gerard Manley Hopkins,* pp. 11–23.
10. John Shaw Neilson, *The Poems of Shaw Neilson,* Angus & Robertson, Sydney, (Lothian Books), 1973.

Reading List

J. B. Phillips, *Your God is Too Small,* Epworth Press, London, 1982.
Etty Hillesum, *A Diary 1941–43,* Triad Panther Books, London, 1983.

3.

'Caught, Not Taught'

When I was first preparing to teach poetry in schools, I asked an experienced Loreto nun how to go about it. She replied, 'Poetry is not taught, it is caught'. This, it seems to me is what the Lord is saying to the disciples when they ask him to teach them to pray.

> Now once he was in a certain place praying and when he had finished, one of his disciples said 'Lord, teach us to pray just as John taught his disciples'. He said to them 'Say this when you pray: Father, may your name be held holy, your kingdom come, give us each day our daily bread and forgive us our sins for we ourselves forgive each one who is in debt to us and do not put us to the test.' (Luke 11: 1–4)

The disciples are drawn to pray by seeing Jesus praying. Having aroused their desire, he is then able to tell them more about prayer.

> He also said to them 'Suppose one of you has a friend and goes to him in the middle of the night to say "My friend, lend me three loaves, because a friend of mine on his travels has just arrived at my house and I have nothing to offer him", and the man answers from inside the house "Do not bother me, the door is bolted now and my children and I are in bed. I cannot get up to give it you." I tell you if the

man does not get up and give it him for friendship's sake, persistence will be enough to make him get up and give his friend all he wants.

'So I say to you, ask and it will be given to you, search and you will find, knock and the door will be open to you. For the one who asks always receives, the one who searches always finds, the one who knocks will always have the door open to him. What father among you would hand his son a stone when he asked for bread or hand him a snake instead of a fish or hand him a scorpion if he asked for an egg? If you then who are evil know how to give your children what is good, how much more will the heavenly Father give the Holy Spirit to those who ask him?' (Luke 11: 5–13)

Only the Lord can teach us to pray. No spiritual directors or gurus teach us to pray. They may help us clear away misconceptions of God, of self or of prayer, may help us to be disposed physically or emotionally to pray, but they cannot teach us to pray, because prayer is a gift that God alone can give, and because entrance into prayer is an act of faith.

So we do what the disciples did. We come before the Lord begging, 'Lord, teach us to pray'. Two things are clear from this: one, that prayer is a gift that God alone can give; and, two, that the key to the art of prayer is petitionary prayer. The hands held out begging, as Tony de Mello used to say, achieve much more than the hands pressed against the head. That second posture suggests effort and much thinking. Prayer is loving, not much thinking, says Teresa of Jesus.

We must wholeheartedly desire this gift. Mark Link in *Breakaway* tells the story of a young man who asked a guru to teach him to pray. At first the guru took no notice, but the man persisted. Then the master grabbed the man and thrust his head under the water of a nearby river. He held him there till he was at his last gasp, and only then released him. When he recovered his breath, the would-be disciple asked why he had been treated so. 'I only asked you to teach me to pray,' he said. 'You've had your first lesson,' was the reply. 'When you desire to pray with the intensity with which you just desired air, you will be on the way.'[1]

Jesus answers the apostles' request by praying with and for them. Growth in prayer comes by praying. Attending courses, reading books and studying of themselves are not enough, but they are helpful if they move us to pray. We learn to pray by praying as we learn to swim by swimming, and to love by loving. Jesus emphasises two qualities, persistence and confidence. The story of the unfortunate friend who gets what he wants through sheer persistence is a good reminder for all who are offering a prayer of petition.

A great enemy of prayer is discouragement. This should not surprise us, since all growth in marriage relationships moves from romance through disillusionment to joy, as Marriage Encounter teaches so beautifully. We can get bogged down in the disillusionment, the discouragement. How often I hear people say 'When I pray, nothing happens', and again, 'I talk to God and he does not answer'. This can be discouraging and yet so often such an experience can be a sign of growth in prayer. 'When I pray, nothing happens' often may mean, 'I have no thoughts. I am thinking nothing. I am doing nothing.' Prayer is not us doing, but God acting. Prayer is not us thinking, but loving. So the discouragement may really be impressing on us the true nature of prayer: that it is the gift of faith, hope and love from the Spirit.

But it may, on the other hand, be caused by our lack of discipline, by our failure in preparation, or by self-centredness. The story is told of a young man who asked a hermit to teach him to pray. 'Why do you want to pray?' the hermit asked him. 'Because that is the highest knowledge' was the reply. And the hermit kindly but firmly sent him away. Some years later the young man asked again. 'Why do you want to pray?' the hermit asked. 'So as to be a saint,' replied the young man. And again he was sent away. A third time he came with his request. His answer now was, 'I want to pray because I want to find God'. And the hermit said, 'You can stay, for now you are ready to begin'.

Discouragement may be caused by anxiety, tension, worry, fatigue—all of which can be barriers to any communication and can hinder a true encounter.

We therefore need to reflect upon the experiences we have in prayer so that we may learn from them. Perseverance in the face of discouragement can be richly rewarded. Reflection on the causes, and determination to keep praying, are called for by this teaching of Jesus. It is most important to allow our feelings to surface and to take them to God. Discouragement can follow the suppression of anger, grieving, fear, and so on.

The teaching about asking, searching and knocking drives home the same message. One of the gifts the Charismatic Renewal has given the Church is to remind it of this trust in prayer, a deep belief in the power of prayer, especially the prayer of praise. I might say that I have no problem with affirming my belief in the power of prayer in general, but I am not so comfortable when speaking about the prayer of another person. It is still more disconcerting when I ask myself—do I really believe in the power of this prayer that I have just offered for that sick person?

Do I expect the Lord will answer me?

When I am honest, I know that sometimes I would be surprised at the Lord answering my prayer! Yet if I really listened to what he says in the Gospel, I should be surprised if he *didn't* answer my prayer.

I like the notion that the Charismatic Renewal uses, of *expectant faith* which, I suppose, could be said to be hope clinging firmly to one's faith. If my expectations of my prayer are pretty low, I need to reflect upon the faith with which I pray. I also need to reflect upon the desire I have when I go to prayer.

Entrance into prayer is an act of faith. Prayer is simply believing that we are living in the mystery of God. This is not the natural awareness that tells me of the sun's heat, or somebody's presence, but an awareness of faith at the very core of my being, acknowledging the mystery of God in my life. The life of prayer is simply allowing God to be present to me and allowing him to make me present to him.

The passage that I quoted earlier from Luke's Gospel records the explicit teaching Jesus gives on prayer. In John's Gospel we find several passages that record the prayer Jesus made to his Father:

> Among those who went up to worship at the festival were some Greeks. These approached Philip who came from Bethsaida in Galilee and put this request to him 'Sir, we should like to see Jesus'. Philip went to tell Andrew, and Andrew and Philip together went to tell Jesus. Jesus replied to them 'Now the hour has come for the son of man to be glorified. I tell you most solemnly, unless a wheat grain falls on the ground and dies, it remains only a single grain, but if it dies, it yields a rich harvest. Anyone who hates his life in this world will keep it for the eternal life. If a man serves me, he must follow me. Wherever I am, my servant will be there too. If anyone serves me, my Father will honour him. Now my soul is troubled, what shall I say: 'Father, save me from this hour? But it was for this very reason that I have come to this hour. Father glorify your name.' A voice came from heaven 'I have glorified it, and I will glorify it again.' (12:20-28)

In a very direct and disconcerting reply, Jesus spells out how we may come to see him and build a relationship with him. It is no different from building up any friendship. If I am to come to know and love another person, I must be prepared to put aside my own personal agenda, to lose myself in him or her. The more I can do that, the deeper will the intimacy be, the truer the encounter. This is a dying to self and absorption in him that Jesus is describing in his metaphor of the seed dying.

But to do this requires self-sacrifice. By way of encouragement, Jesus promises the reward of being honoured by the Father. There is further insight as Jesus also reveals to us the struggle in his own soul, as he is reminded of his own coming Passion and death. He comes to peace by moving toward his Father.

By sharing himself so intimately with us, Jesus illustrates by his own example how we build deeper relationships with one another and also with him. The journey into love is made by fully surrendering oneself to new life.

But the most explicit and certainly the longest prayer that we have in John's Gospel is the priestly prayer of Jesus given in Chapter 17, which commences 'Father, the hour has come. Glorify your son so that your son may glorify you and through the power over all mankind that you have given him, let him give eternal life to those you have entrusted to him'. We notice that this prayer begins precisely in the same way as the prayer instruction in Luke's Gospel. It begins by being present to the Father, and that is always to be the beginning of prayer, that action of becoming aware of God's presence.

When I was a novice, we were instructed to 'put ourselves in the presence of God'. That is not a phrase that appeals to me now, because I know that I am always in the presence of God and that I don't have to put myself there. But I also know that I am not always aware of that truth. So now I prefer the advice, 'Be aware of being present to God, and of God being present to you, at the beginning of your prayer'.

You will notice too, that in this prayer by Jesus, as in the Our Father, there is a movement out toward others. There is petition, there is praise, there is a familiar discourse or conversation with the Father. It's like two friends talking about the mission of Jesus. Jesus is, as it were, reporting back to his Father, and he is also pleading with the Father for his followers.

This chapter 17 is a part of scripture that well rewards thoughtful reflection and a leisurely reading aloud of the prayer.

Reflections

1. Read aloud slowly the passage from Luke 11 quoted at the beginning of this chapter, and consider the following questions:

   (a) What does the passage tell you about the relationship between Jesus and his Father?

(b) What does it say about *your* relationship with Jesus and with the Father?
(c) What is Jesus teaching about the nature of prayer and the dispositions for prayer?

2. Prayer sometimes means wrestling with God.

(a) In John 12, what struggle do you see going on within Jesus?
(b) How is it resolved?
(c) Does this tell you anything about who Jesus is?

3. Read aloud slowly chapter 17 of John's Gospel.

(a) What is the tone of the prayer?
(b) Linger on any part that appeals to you.

4. The extract from chapter 12 of John's Gospel speaks of death leading to life.

(a) Can you recall any time when a friendship was renewed or revitalised by your willingness to forget your rights?
(b) Can you recall a prayer experience in which your faith, hope and love were strengthened?
(c) Reflect on that experience to discover how God was meeting you and leading you.

5. Play the song by Joe Wise, 'Lord, Teach Us to Pray' (*A New Day*, Fontaine House).

(a) Reflect on the teaching about integrating living and praying. Which stanza recalls a barrier in your own life?
(b) Reflect on areas of your life or attitudes that need to be harmonised with your prayer.
(c) Talk this over with Jesus.

6. Play the tape, 'Lose Yourself in Me,' by Carey Landrey (*I Will Never Forget You,* North American Liturgy Resources, Phoenix, Arizona).

Reflect upon any thoughts and feelings that you experience while listening.

Notes

1. Mark Link SJ, *Breakaway*, Argus Communications, Allen, Texas, 1980.

Reading List

George A. Maloney SJ, *Lord, Teach Us to Pray*, Gabriel Publishing Company, Inc., 1981.

Jean Laplace SJ, *Prayer According to the Scriptures*, Religious of the Cenacle, Brighton, Massachusetts, n.d.

Karl Rahner SJ, *On Prayer*, Paulist Press, New York, 1968.

Rhonda Chervin, *Prayer and Your Everyday Life*, Ligouri Publications, Ligouri, Missouri, n.d.

Abhishiktananda, *Prayer*, SPCK, London, 1972.

4.

Drawn—or Driven?

When I was a novice we were called at the crack of dawn every morning. We hastened to the chapel for morning prayer and then spent an hour in meditation. I am not sure whether we were drawn to prayer or driven—probably a bit of both.

Ideally I should be *drawn* to pray, rather than *driven.* Reflection on why I pray may give me the answer and help me reach for the ideal.

The first recorded words of Jesus in John's Gospel are spoken to his disciples. They are following him, and he says to them 'What do you want?' They reply 'Where do you live?' He answers 'Come and see' (John 1: 35-39). That little scene can be helpful as we explore our own prayer journey. What am I looking for when I pray? Do I pray mostly out of a sense of obligation, as though I feel driven to it? Or when I'm in great need? Is my prayer time a time I look forward to?

We pray, of course, to give thanks to God for all his gifts, to praise him for his goodness, to appeal to him in our needs, to ask pardon because of our sinfulness and to make up for our own failures in relationships.

But why do *I* pray? If I consider the general aims of prayer which is the one that most applies to *my* prayer? Is mine usually a prayer of praise, a prayer of petition, a prayer of thanksgiving, a prayer of sorrow or a prayer of atonement? Most of us don't always consider this when we begin prayer. For many of us, prayer may be just routine, and we reflect only rarely on why we pray. Yet growth in prayerfulness may be assisted by considering, more personally, what are the motives that bring me to prayer?

Most schoolteachers are aware of the urgent prayer that is prompted by examination fever. Students, sometimes very worried, go to God for help. One often wonders whether, after the examination results have come out, the prayer of thanksgiving is equally as heartfelt.

It is certainly true that there are occasions when we feel driven to pray because of deep anxiety, deep sorrow, deep care for others in times of bereavement, in times of our own sickness or the sickness of those we love. In times of deep distress for ourselves or for others, we go to God and pray earnestly. On such occasions, prayer tends to be intense and spontaneous, but on other occasions our prayer will not have that same spontaneity or intensity. Prayer tends to rise out of our own needs. It is surely consoling that we are drawn to turn to God in these times of stress.

True friends, however, wish to share not only sorrows but also joys. They also like being with one another to enjoy their love, and so intimacy grows. The same holds for the relationship I have with God. Do I go to him seriously only in time of stress? By considering when, why and how I pray, I can be helping the growth of my intimacy with my God. Do I pray out of a sense of duty, out of fear, when I am driven by obligation and guilt? The answers I give to these questions may help me clarify who my God is.

I recall an incident, many years ago. It was getting close to midnight. I had not finished my obligatory 'Office', or 'prayer for the day'. I saw that if I hurried, I could get it all said by midnight, and so satisfy that particular rule for priests. The thought came to me that if I said it slowly and prayerfully, I would not get it finished. What should I do? I decided to say it slowly and prayerfully and accept that the obligation to finish it by midnight would not be fulfilled.

That decision gave me a great sense of freedom. I think it showed me that my God was not a God who needed to be prayed to compulsively, but a God of compassion. Further reflection upon that experience helped me to see that I could have been praying out of a sense of duty to a God who would be displeased with me unless I fulfilled my obligation.

His grace, however, helped me not to pray out of a sense of duty, but to pray lovingly. Therefore my God was not so much a God imposing an obligation upon me, as a God who was compassionate and loving.

Sometimes now, I reflect upon how my prayer involves God: am I praying *for* him, *at* him, *to* him or *with* him? I can often see that I am doing one or another of these. I hope that, with his grace, I will pray more and more to him and with him, rather than for him or at him.

I need to ask myself, what am I seeking when I pray? This is the question that Jesus posed: 'What do you want?' Am I seeking a happy experience of prayer? Am I seeking the consolation of God, as Francis de Sales put it, or am I seeking the God of the consolations? Am I seeking peace and security?

In his novel *The Book of Lights,* Chaim Potok tells of the rabbi who asks his God for the grace of insecurity. When I read that, I admit I was surprised, and then the deep realisation came that his prayer was genuine. Insecurity can bring about that emptiness that leaves space for God to become one's true support. St Paul discovered this: he was led to accept that when he was weak, he was strong.

Often I find that my prayer can be very self-centred because I am concerned with the things I need and want. At the end of John's Gospel, when Jesus meets Mary Magdalene at the tomb, his question is no longer 'What do you want?' but 'Who is it you want?' I think it spells growth in prayerfulness when we home in on the 'who' rather than the 'what'.

Do I come to prayer looking for solutions, for answers, for information, as though God were an enquiry office whose business it was to provide me with information? No doubt at the beginning of our prayer, we will often see God in that light, but I think our relationship with him deepens when we are praying to encounter God rather than just to ask for his gifts. When there are moments when we appreciate the giver more than the gift, we are beginning to lose ourselves in God. On such occasions we come to love God and to be loved by God. The reality behind the gifts takes over our lives as our prayer becomes less self-centred.

Do I come to prayer to complain ('Lord why have you done this to me?') to explain, to apologise, to question, to rage? Any one of these motives may, at times, move us into prayer, but if I discover that these are the only motives that I ever bring to my relationship with God, I need to reflect upon who my God is. In an earlier chapter I spoke of discovering the God behind the things that happen, the events that occur in our lives. I spoke of the freedom that comes when we discover the God behind the masks that we have created for him.

In retreat work, over the last few years, I have noticed that people are becoming more comfortable with expressing their anger towards God. That, I think, is a healthy growth, as it means that our communication is authentic. We can come before God exactly as we are at that moment. I am able to tell God of my loneliness, my anger, my sexual frustrations, my disappointments. There is no virtue in pretending that these are not part of me, if they preoccupy me at the time I enter prayer.

Authentic prayer that leads to a true encounter can only happen when I am truly myself, but I think there is further growth when I can allow God to be truly God. Not only must I take off my own masks, but I must take off the masks that I or others have put upon my God. When, therefore, I can go beyond complaining to God about my anger towards him; when I have the desire that Etty Hillesum expresses in her diary, and in the letters from Westerbork, to comfort God, my prayer is being purified of my own self-interest.

Etty says 'Poor God, he is so helpless, we must comfort him'[1]. This remarkable prophet of our times, suffering so terribly in the Westerbork concentration camp, does not feel anger towards her God, does not fall into the trap of asking why. '*Why* is this happening to me? *Why* don't you do something about it?'—*why* is always, or nearly always, the wrong question to ask, because it betrays an assumption that God is accountable to us. With the true wisdom given to her by the Spirit of God, Etty Hillesum could see God loving her even in her dire situation, and she could see too, clearly, that God is helpless to change the situation unless he is to destroy what he created: people with free will.

Questions such as these may help me discover the God I pray to, and how I approach God in my prayer. It is so easy to manipulate God, to depersonalise him, to idolise him. Authentic prayer takes place when I can allow God to be God and I myself to be myself. A true encounter with God will want to leave God to be free. But the only way I can leave the other, whether God or a human friend, free is when I forget about myself and lose myself in our relationship. This, I think, is the message that Jesus taught when the Greeks said 'We want to see Jesus' and Jesus told the parable about the grain of wheat that must die before it can bear much fruit. Relationships flourish when I am more concerned about the other person than about myself. As I lose myself in the other, I truly discover myself.

What are my expectations when I pray? It is helpful to distinguish between hopes and expectations. Broadly speaking, hopes are what I want from my prayer. If I pray for somebody who is sick, I hope the person will get better. If I pray for world peace, I hope for peace throughout the world. Expectations are the results that I think will follow. For example, I may hope to go to Lourdes, but my expectations of getting there may not be very high. Exploring the expectations that I have about my prayer may lead me more deeply into the mystery of encountering God.

My expectations may be high, low or unreal. I have met people whose expectations are very high. I remember the mother of a boy being told by a doctor that he would have to operate and remove the boy's left eye to save the sight of the right eye. The mother refused to give her permission. She said, 'I have faith in prayer'. The operation was not performed, and the boy recovered 90 per cent of sight in the bad eye and 100 per cent in the good eye. I am not saying that doctors' advice should be ignored, only that the mother's expectations of her prayer were very, very high.

I recall another case of a girl in Melbourne who wanted to go up to a Charismatic Renewal meeting in Sydney, but she had no money. She said, 'I will get there, The Spirit will get us the money'. I met her at the meeting. 'How did you get here? Where did you get the money?' I asked. 'I had a bet on the TAB,' she replied, 'and here we are.' She had what the Charismatics teach, the gift of *expectant faith*. She expected her prayers to be answered.

It is a wonderful gift from God to have that high expectation; it is not something that we can condition ourselves to, this gift of expectant faith. It is something we pray for, trusting that God keeps his promises. We may need to meditate seriously on the passage in Luke 11, 'Ask and you shall receive', so that we may receive this gift of expectant faith. As Paul says, it is God's power working in us.

My involvement in the healing ministry has led me more deeply into the mystery of expectant faith. In general, I think it would be true to say that we believe our prayers are answered, or at least that prayer is answered. But when I make the question more personal, I ask: Do I believe that *my* prayers will be answered? Do I believe that *this* prayer that I just said for *this* sick person suffering from cancer will be answered? Then I am challenged about the expectations of my prayer and my trust in God. How strong is my belief that in individual cases God will hear my prayer?

Once I used to pray, 'Lord if it is your will, heal this person here'.

I wasn't too happy with the 'if it is your will' bit, because that seemed to be a cop out for a lack of faith. On many occasions, when I have been leading a group in the contemplation of the healing of the leper in Luke 5, I have been struck by the reaction of Jesus to the leper who says 'Sir, if you want to, you can heal me'. 'Of course I want to,' says Jesus. With my head I know that God always answers prayer, but discovering with the heart is not so simple.

I have come to see that God always answers prayers for healing, but I have also accepted that how he heals and when he heals must be left to him. No longer, then, do I pray, 'If you want to, you can heal me'. I no longer separate God's power and love. I see they are one. So now I pray, 'Lord, heal me or others according to your will'. It is true, I know, that I am often surprised when the prayers are answered, whereas if I truly and deeply trusted God I would be surprised if they were *not* answered. This movement into expectant faith is growth in trust and confidence in a God who keeps his promises. 'Lord, I do believe; help my unbelief' becomes a very real plea.

The distinction then between hopes and expectations can open up for us a journey into a deeper, stronger trust in God. When that grace is given us, certainly we have moved a long way from prayer being a performance, something we *do*. Prayer becomes an encounter with God as he really is. Earlier, I wrote of the necessity of accepting that God is more concerned with being present to us in suffering, and that he seems to prefer changing us and our attitudes, and giving us strength, hope and patience, to changing situations. When we meet this God ever present in time of trouble, and stop looking for the God with the magic wand, we are allowing ourselves to be drawn into the paschal mystery and to meet God who is love. As Julian of Norwich said, 'Love is his meaning'.

In his book, *The Way of the Heart*, Henri Nouwen makes a distinction between compulsive ministry and compassionate ministry.[2] Compulsive ministry means that I am driven by a sense of guilt, whereas the compassionate type is motivated by love. We may apply the same distinction to prayer. Compulsive prayer is a performance triggered off by 'ought' and 'should'. Prayer of compassion is a true encounter that flows from love. I pray not because I ought to, but because I want to.

Reflections

1. The story of my journey with God

   Context

   'I know the plans I have in mind for you—it is Yahweh who speaks—plans for peace, not disaster, reserving a future full of hope for you. Then when you call to me, I will listen to you. When you seek me you shall find me, when you seek me with all your heart, I will let you find me.' (Jeremiah 29: 11-13)

   I read through these words slowly and imagine the Lord telling me of his plans for me and my life.

   Grace

   I ask for the grace to discover how God has been present to me during the years and to respond more generously to this love of God flooding my heart.

   Method

   There are different ways of reflecting on your life journey and God. Use any way you wish.

   - It may be just a leisurely path through the stages of your life, talking over the events with Jesus.
   - Return to any experience when God seemed close to you. In your imagination recapture the occasion with vivid detail so that you relive it again. Note the feelings you have and rest in them.
   - Recapture and relive a time of struggle in your life that involved an invitation to repentance, or a new way of living.
   - Read through the Emmaus story (Luke 24: 13-35) and reflect on your journey.
   - Take Psalm 23 (The Lord is my Shepherd) to help you recall ways the Lord has been with you.

   Colloquy

   I talk over with the Lord whatever comes to me, as one friend talks to another.

   I close with an Our Father.

2. 'Why' questions easily lead to blaming, such as 'Why has God done this to me? Why has he allowed this to happen?' God is made

responsible, accountable to us. Notice the difference when we rephrase the question: 'In what way is God loving me through this?' Here the basic assumption is that God is a loving, not a punishing or demanding God.

3. Consider the difference between 'How can I please God?', 'How can I placate him?', 'How can I love him?' Which statement would usually describe your approach to God?

4. Reflect upon the nature and qualities of a prayer of praise, such as Glory be to the Father, Glory to God in the highest.

5. Read Mary's *Magnificat* (Luke 1: 46–55). Now write out your own prayer of praise and thanksgiving.

Notes

1. Etty Hillesum, *A Diary*, pp. 192, 197
2. Henri J. M. Nouwen, *The Way of The Heart*, Darton, Longman & Todd, London, 1981.

Reading List

Henri J. M. Nouwen, *The Way of The Heart*, Darton, Longman & Todd, London, 1981.

Robert Ochs SJ, *God is More Present Than You Think*, Paulist Press, New York, 1970.

Thomas H. Green SJ, *Opening to God*, Ave Maria Press, Notre Dame, Indiana, 1977.

Mark Link SJ, *You—Prayer for Beginners*, Argus Communications, Allen, Texas, 1976.

Archbishop Anthony Bloom, *Living Prayer*, A Libra Book, 1966.

5.

Feelings— Friends or Enemies?

Many of us can become quite confused about feelings and prayer. 'On no account let your feelings influence your prayer' was common advice once. As in living, so in praying, our feelings were suppressed. Then there came the 'feeling revolution', with the pioneering work of Freud and the depth psychologists. We were told that feelings may not be ignored, that in our living, loving and praying, we should be aware of our feelings. How do we reconcile two seemingly contradictory viewpoints?

I believe there is wisdom in both. The earlier teaching, especially in relation to prayer, was that feelings should not decide whether you pray. The attitude, 'I'll pray if I feel like it, and I won't pray when I don't feel like it', was being attacked. I'll love you when I feel like it, I'll work when I feel like it—this stance, too, was seen as wrong. Importance was attached to the will and to being above feelings, able to decide on intellectual grounds. Our mentors, therefore, were correct when understood in this way.

But I also see wisdom in the frequent teaching of these times that stresses the importance of listening to our feelings. When we do that, we learn a great deal about ourselves and our attitudes. This awareness and acceptance of our feelings can help our prayer, because feelings play an important part in communication and behaviour.

So often in a Marriage Encounter Weekend I have seen the power of that sharing of feelings between husband and wife. Many do not find it easy to be in touch with their feelings. After a little while, they are able to do that, and gradually they come to trust each other with this precious gift of who they are. For feelings are a very important part of the person, though not the whole. Being in touch with them, sharing them, deepens the relationship. This is true also of our relationship with God.

A clearer idea of feelings will help us to see their importance in prayer. A feeling is a spontaneous response to a person or a situation. If it is just bodily, it is a physical sensation: thus, I feel hungry, cold, tired. When this involuntary response is more than physical, it is concerned with our humanness: I feel sad, angry, glad, scared. It is this kind of response that needs to be understood in the discussion about prayer.

The physical sensation is a message to me about my physical needs. The hunger tells me that I need food. If I completely ignore the message, I'll die. The pain in my tooth tells me that the tooth is in trouble. Ignore it and I will lose the tooth.

Involuntary human responses, called feelings, are messages to me about not only my physical needs, but also my emotional needs. My emotional needs are: to be loved, to love, to be wanted, to belong, to be free. If any of these are not being met, distress signals are sent up. If they *are* being met, we feel that all is well. If I am rejected, I experience fear, anger, loneliness. The stronger the rejection, the more intense the feelings.

Feelings then are messages to me, about me. When I ignore them I'm like a person who takes the phone off the hook. By being attentive to these messages, however, and by acknowledging them, I can then decide what should be done.

I belong to a Healing Group which meets every Thursday. We celebrate Mass and then pray quietly over whoever wants prayer and the laying on of hands. All participate by silently praying. The mood is very low key.

Once when I was laying hands on somebody, a lady who was a visitor joined me and began praying in the insistent loud way that some charismatic groups adopt. I became aware of my irritation and anger, but I continued praying silently, accepting my angry feeling. Gradually I began to see what my anger was telling me: that I thought my way of praying was better than hers, that the Spirit would listen to all of us, not to her. Still staying with the anger while I continued to pray, I saw that my attitude was judgmental, in that I was not letting God be God. I accepted the message from my feelings about this unloving attitude. I asked the Lord to heal me. Then I noted that the anger went away and I could pray peacefully with our visitor. My feeling of anger had revealed to me a deeply hidden lack of freedom and it had left me when the message was received.

Another time, as I noted a feeling of anxiety arising within, I began to reflect that I was not God and not called to be Saviour of the world. This was a deeply liberating experience.

In my retreat work I am called to do much listening. I find that if I also note how I feel, I obtain insights into the other person, and a relaxing sense of being free, which helps me listen better.

Feelings are therefore important because they tell me of my needs, reveal hidden attitudes, and act like a fuse block, as the positive ones say the relationship is okay, and the so-called negative ones warn me that something is amiss. So they are both life giving.

Feelings, as such, have no morality—they are neither right nor wrong. Feeling happy does not, of itself, make me a good person. Neither does feeling sad, or feeling angry, make me a bad person. It is behaviour in its fullness that is either right or wrong, good or bad. Many believe that it is sinful to be angry, because anger is one of the seven deadly sins. We need to distinguish between angry feelings and angry behaviour. Constructive use of the angry feeling will help control angry behaviour.

When couples in a Marriage Encounter Weekend understand this, they are helped in their communication, and this deeper communication develops their relationship.

As we have seen, the lifeblood of our relationship with God is communication. Since feelings are an important part of me, I need to be aware of them, and I must acknowledge them as my own: *I* am angry, *I* am afraid, and so on.

Next I must be free enough to tell God this. If my God is unable to handle my anger, or my fear, then he is too small. He cannot be the God of scripture who loves me unconditionally. For a clearer understanding of the value of this trusting openness, I suggest reading *May I Hate God?* by Pierre Wolff.[1]

Feelings, then, are our friends, not our enemies. They should never be our masters. Welcome them, acknowledge them as friends, and you will discover their power to help you grow in relationship with God. As you become aware of, and welcome, the feelings that arise in your prayer, you will be moving the prayer from the head to the heart. This will develop affective prayer, which is the prayer of the affections and is a way to simple, non-discursive contemplation.

Reflections

1. How do you *feel* when Jesus says, 'Come follow me and forgive your enemies'? No doubt you will have thoughts about the invitation. For example, you might *think* that Jesus wants you to leave your present job. Or you might *think* that if you forgive your boss, who has it in for you, he will walk all over you. These are legitimate intellectual responses. Underneath them are 'feeling' responses. What are they? What are they saying about your emotional needs? What will you do about them? A rewarding prayer might be to talk over all these questions with Jesus, or the Father, or the Spirit.

2. How do you *feel* when Jesus takes your few loaves and fish and feeds the multitude, and there are twelve basketfuls left over?

3. What do you think Jesus *felt* (not thought) when Judas kissed him, when Peter denied him, when he heard that Judas had committed suicide, when the Good Thief said, 'Jesus, remember me'?

4. What do you *feel* when Jesus says to you, 'Come to me when you are heavily burdened and I will refresh you'?

   By being aware of your thoughts and your feelings, you are discovering more about your hidden self, and allowing it to grow stronger.

5. O Lamps of fire!
In whose splendors
The deep caverns of feeling,
Once obscure and so blind,

Now give forth, so rarely, so exquisitely,
Both warmth and light to their Beloved.
(St John of the Cross, 'The Living Flame of Love')[2]

Sit quietly with these lines from the poem of the great Spanish mystic and Doctor of the Church.

Notes

1. Pierre Wolff, *May I Hate God?* Paulist Press, New York, 1979.
2. St John of the Cross, *The Collected Works of St John of The Cross,* ICS Publications, Washington DC, 1979, p. 717.

Reading List

Willard Gaylin, *Feelings,* Ballantine Books, New York, 1980.
Paul Tournier, *Guilt and Grace,* Hodder & Stoughton, London, 1974.
Jules J. Toner SJ, *A Commentary on St Ignatius' Rules for the Discernment of Spirits,* The Institute of Jesuit Sources, St Louis, 1982.
Conrad W. Baars MD, *Feeling and Healing Your Emotions,* Logos International, Plainfield, New Jersey, 1979.
Harriet Goldhor Lerner, *The Dance of Anger,* Perennial Library, Harper & Row, New York, 1986.
Anger, The Tenth Psychotheological Symposium, Affirmation Books, Natick, Massachusetts, 1985.

6.

Surprise Discoveries Start with Listening

Any genuine encounter is a complex experience that involves listening, learning, loving and living. This holds true whether it is a face-to-face meeting with God, partner, children or friends. An encounter that is a 'surprise discovery' challenges our present self-understanding as well as our future goals. It is much more than a controlled, structured and predictable meeting. Discovering God or another in depth disarms us, exposes our masks and pretences, calls us 'to launch out into the deep', to let go of safe structures, to surrender in trust to the presence of the other.

Notice how Jesus could turn a human meeting into an encounter. Zaccheus, the Samaritan woman at the well, the suffering woman who touched the hem of his garment—all experienced the surprise discovery of Jesus and themselves. For the encounter to take place, they needed openness, trust, self-awareness and honesty about themselves. These are the prerequisites for the type of encounter that led them to discover Jesus loving them into life, and so profoundly changing them.

As we reflect on their experiences, we see the consequences of an encounter. There is a conversion, a change of heart, and the grace of this conversion flows from every true encounter. This in turn leads them to reach out to others—Zaccheus to the poor, the Samaritan woman to bear witness in front of the crowd.

In Mark 3 the healing of a man with a withered hand is described:

> Jesus went again into a synagogue, and there was a man there who had a withered hand. And they were watching him to see if he would cure him on the sabbath day, hoping for something to use against him. He said to the man with the withered hand, 'Stand up out in the middle'. Then he said to them, 'Is it against the law on the sabbath day to do good, or to do evil; to save life, or to kill?' But they said nothing. Then, grieved to find them so obstinate, he looked angrily round at them, and said to the man, 'Stretch out your hand'. He stretched it out and his hand was better. The Pharisees went out and at once began to plot with the Herodians against him, discussing how to destroy him.

The sick man is open and trusting, prepared to expose himself not only to Jesus, but also to those hostile to Jesus. So he stands out in front and stretches out the withered hand. Being so open to the healing love of Jesus, he is restored to health. There has been a true encounter between them.

The Pharisees are hostile and their hearts are withered, as they reveal neither compassion for the sick man nor openness to Jesus. He moves to meet them in depth with his question about saving life, or killing. They remain silent because they are obstinately fixed against change and growth. It is a chilling thought that they unite with the Herodians to kill Jesus, and it is the Sabbath. Since they lack openness, trust, self-awareness and honesty, no encounter takes place. Death is all that results.

Jesus reveals himself. He is sad as he grieves over his failure to reach these men. He is angry because he loves them and he wishes to heal their withered hearts and lead them into a true conversion experience. His failure to do this, however, does not close him off from the sick man.

To him, to the people there, and to us he reveals his healing power of love. As we reflect on this scene and many others like it, we see again that prayer means listening, learning, loving, living—with listening as the start of it all.

Every entry into prayer is an act of faith. There is, in some way or another, an awareness of God's presence to me and my presence to God. This is not any kind of sensory awareness, as when I am aware of the sun and its heat, but an awareness of faith. I am exercising my conviction that I am living in the mystery of God, that all creation is simply God communicating himself to me. There is awareness of God's presence, a listening to the God who is present, a personal response to my God. And that is prayer.

All true listening begins with being aware of the other and moves towards being lost in the other. The deeper the listening, the deeper the intimacy of self-giving. This is listening to *accept*—not to *judge*, not to *evaluate*, not to *use*, but just to receive the other person. In so doing, I give more than time to the other; I draw that person into my life, as he, she, or God draws me into their life. The depths of the giving and receiving, the listening and the responding indicate the intimacy of the relationship.

Prayer is just such a listening experience. I listen to God loving me, I listen to my responses to God loving me. God listens to me and responds to me. The giving and receiving dynamism of the Eucharist embodies this dance of love: our words go up to God and his words come down to us; at the offertory we begin a new dance as our gifts go up to God and his gifts come down to us.

Some time ago a troubled lady, whom I was trying to help, committed suicide. I was shocked and distressed, and felt much anger, grieving, and guilt. When I tried to talk about this, I was told not to feel guilty, and that I had done all that was possible; there was no need to blame myself. My head knew all this, but knowledge was not enough. When I talked to a friend about my feelings, my guilt, my self-blame, she just listened, without in any way judging, advising, or rejecting. It was a consoling experience of being accepted, and her true listening began to heal me.

Despite that, I still had a sense of unfinished business, a feeling that the healing needed to be deepened. So I asked Jesus how he felt when he heard that Judas had committed suicide. 'Did you fall into the anguish of "If only . . ."?' I asked. As I tried to enter into the mystery of the relationship between Jesus and Judas, I began to sense acceptance, and even though the pain of the loss remained, the somewhat selfish preoccupation with my own reactions left me.

Both my friend and Jesus seemed to me to be listening in an accepting way and loving me. My prayer was a listening experience.

During a Marriage Encounter Weekend, listening in a loving, accepting way is a theme that is presented. We reflect on the parable of the Sower to see how well we are listening. We also see that rejecting the partner's feelings, or even just tolerating them is not listening with acceptance. I know that my weekend and continued work in Marriage

Encounter have helped me to listen and accept my feelings as well as those of others. This acceptance and the emphasis on the affections have helped my prayer. Many couples in the journey toward each other, toward God, and then together toward God, have felt the same.

True prayer is personal. As our prayer, that is, our communication with God develops, we experience growth in intimacy. When I say 'God made the world', I am talking *about* God. This is impersonal and, as it stands, just a fact, not a prayer. When I say 'God made me', I am still talking about God, but it is now personal. Yet it is hardly communication. When I say 'God, you made me', I am talking to God and so am being more personal. With 'Father, you are creating me now', I am still talking to God, but the emotions suggested by 'Father', bring in more affection and intimacy.

So far, however, all this is a monologue. For true communication, prayer, we need dialogue. Talking to God is an advance on talking about God, but until we are talking with God, we have no dialogue. There is dialogue when I also listen to what God communicates to me, when I hear God. This does not mean hearing actual voices, which John of the Cross warns against listening for, but an awareness of my thoughts and my feelings as coming from God.

Thus I say, 'Father, you are loving life into me now'. As I think of that, I may feel grateful, loved, amazed, secure, I may rest with that sense of God's love, or I may be moved to thank God, to tell him I love him and so on. The dialogue, the dance, has begun. God and I are communicating with each other.

St Teresa said that prayer is not much talking or thinking, but much loving. As the movement is from *about* God and *to* God towards *with* God, space is made for the personal response of love.

An analogy can be made here with the communication expressed by sex. Is sex to be *to* your partner, *for* your partner, or *with* your partner? There is the mutual loving of an intimate relationship only when the two persons have sex *with* each other. Prayer, too, is not *about* God, or even *for* God, or something I do *to* God, but a loving relationship *with* God.

If I am to listen to God, I must become still. 'Be still and know that I am God.' At the beginning of prayer, I quiet my body by becoming still—a physical stillness—in the posture that best suits me for prayer. Then I begin to slow down my mind and my imagination, so that I can be freed from my preoccupations. Some people are helped by doing awareness exercises. Others more readily enter into stillness by just becoming silent.

The silence deep within is God's country. As I journey inwards, I find him there. Simone Weil said that the basis of the spiritual life is to wait patiently but with expectation for the coming of the Lord. Perhaps I am reading sacred scripture slowly, attentively, and some word or phrase strikes me. Then I pause. At first nothing may seem to happen but instead of becoming discouraged, I wait with expectant faith.

It is much like going into a dark room. At first I can see nothing, but then as my eyes adjust to the darkness, shapes begin to emerge clearly. So as I adjust to the silence, I begin to hear the silent music described by John of the Cross. This may be a gentle sense of peace or God's presence or a warmth drawing me to God. Often I heard Tony de Mello say: 'Muddy water, let be, will become clear.' Pauline McKinnon tells how she was healed of agoraphobia by meditation that led her into stillness.[1]

A common barrier to listening is a misunderstanding of the nature of prayer. If I wrongly think it means much talking, thinking, imaginative activity, I shall leave no space for listening. The words 'Be still and know that I am God' and 'Silence is the great revelation' express truths that enable us to nourish the contemplative attitude.

When I am very active and allow no space for slowing down, it is very difficult for me to hear the 'silent music' of God's love. By developing a contemplative attitude to life and a sense of wonder at the mystery of God communicating himself to me in his world, I can more easily enter into silence.

Discouragement may trouble me. Often I have heard it said, 'When I stop to listen, I hear nothing'. Sometimes this may mean that nothing is happening in the head—there are no thoughts. At times, as we have talked about this, we have become aware that there is a gentle peace. A lot may be happening in the heart. Or it may be that I am being schooled in patience, being taught to slow down. Perhaps I am the victim of my self-fulfilling prophecies because I do not expect anything to happen.

Reflections such as these show that it is not true to say that nothing happens. Much is happening. Perhaps by asking myself how I am feeling when nothing happens in my prayer, I may discover my anger, or my discouragement, or my disappointment in myself, or my self-blame. This I can then bring to the Lord.

Reflection on the idea that 'nothing happens when I pray' can lead to a deep encounter with my Lord God. Then my lack of expectant faith, or my poor preparation for prayer, or my fear of the 'self-emptying' of silence, is revealed to me. It may be that I am unwilling to let God take over, and that I am clinging to the controls.

Listening to the experience can prove very rewarding, as it leads us to learn about ourselves and God and our relationship. Thus we are led into loving ourselves and God, and reaching out to others, choosing life and death. His seeming absence may deepen our longing, our hunger for him. As Gibran the Prophet says, absence deepens love by intensifying the desire for the beloved.[2] In the Songs of Songs, the beloved seeks for the one who has wounded her heart. The longing for the seemingly absent Jesus expresses the presence of the Spirit in the darkness. We cannot hunger for our God unless the Spirit of God is dwelling within.

Another barrier to the stillness of listening can be comparisons with others. I begin to compare how I am praying with the way somebody else prays, and usually to my detriment: 'I wish I could pray the way so-and-so prays. He or she is so absorbed. God is surely more pleased with that prayer than mine. If only I could pray as well.' The real mistake here is that I see my prayer as a performance. This brings my focus away from God and onto what I am doing. Thus an encounter is prevented, as I do not allow God to act freely with me.

This form of 'image praying' often reflects the fact that I am afraid to be myself because of my preoccupation with pleasing others. Over-emphasis on people-pleasing and God-pleasing flows over into my prayer. I become anxious about pleasing God.

Once I was talking with a couple who were struggling with their marriage. When the wife asked what her husband would like for dinner, or what TV show he would like to watch, or whether they should go out, he invariably replied, 'What would *you* like, dear?' As we talked, it became very clear that he was afraid to express his preference lest she be displeased with him. It was equally clear that she was becoming more and more frustrated. As they talked about this and each could see what was happening to their relationship, he was able to let go of his fear of displeasing her and to reveal his real desires.

People-pleasers and God-pleasers let fear dominate their living and their praying. We must learn to be our own person. The true revelation of the self builds up a trusting love, and so living and praying are nourished. The way I relate to people will mirror the way I relate to God.

Reflections

1. Think of an occasion when you felt your partner, children or a friend really listened to you. Recall the experience as fully as you can. What are your feelings?

2. Consider the difference between listening in preparation for a rebuttal and listening with a view to acceptance. How do you listen in your prayer? How do you think God listens to your prayer?

3. Here are some descriptions of listening:

   Listening with your eyes.
   Listening to the non-verbal communication.
   Listening to what is not said.

   Reflect upon a religious experience and see if any of these descriptions apply to your listening, and God's listening, in that experience.

4. Read the following attentively and slowly. What are your thoughts and feelings?

   And so I saw most surely that it is quicker for us and easier for us to come to the knowledge of God than it is to know our own soul. For our soul is so deeply grounded in God and so endlessly treasured that we cannot come to the knowledge of it until we first have knowledge of God, who is the Creator to whom it is united—Julian of Norwich.

   Let nothing disturb thee,
   Let nothing afright thee
   All things pass.
   God never changes—St Teresa.

   Interior prayer costs nothing but the effort to sink down in silence into the depths of one's heart and call more and more on the radiant name of Jesus—*The Way of the Pilgrim.*

5. A prayer about listening:

   God, you are the best listener I know. You listen the way a lover listens, being totally and actively present to me, always available and never too busy, always accepting me even if you cannot approve of all that I do.

So your listening gives me hope and strength and helps me to face life.

Help me to listen with my heart to others so that they too may experience hope and strength, and the sense of being worth listening to.

Notes

1. Pauline McKinnon, *In Stillness Conquer Fear,* Dove Communications, Blackburn, Victoria, 1978.
2. Kahlil Gibran, *The Prophet,* Heinemann, London, 1970, p. 8.

Reading List

Gerard W. Hughes, *God of Surprises,* Darton, Longman & Todd, London, 1985.
Michael Buckley DD, *Let Peace Disturb You,* Collins Fount Paperbacks, London, 1985.
John Shea, *Stories of God,* The Thomas More Press, Chicago, Illinois, 1978.
R. M. French, *The Way of a Pilgrim,* SPCK, London, 1972.

7.

The Crazy Lover

St Catherine of Siena calls God a crazy lover who, contemplating the beauty of all creation, fell madly in love with it. Contemplation has that power of making us fall in love.

The word 'contemplation' is used, however, with different meanings by different writers. Very often it means mystical prayer, as in the writings of John of the Cross, Teresa of Jesus, and others. Ignatius Loyola seems to use it in different ways, too. At one stage he speaks about contemplating a scene from scripture, and this is a form of prayer that belongs particularly to the *Spiritual Exercises*.

It is a prayer that leads to prayer of the heart, praying in one's own words, slowing down the mind and imagination. Finally one may rest with the prayer, just looking or listening. The climax of the *Spiritual Exercises* of Ignatius Loyola is the 'Contemplation for Attaining Divine Love', a Trinitarian prayer that moves freely with the mind and the imagination in search of the immanent God.

Ignatius learnt to contemplate the scriptural scenes from his reading, and he popularised the method through his *Spiritual Exercises.* So I will speak of scriptural contemplation to distinguish it from other forms of contemplation, and to specify the contemplations given in the *Exercises.*

Its essential quality is to become present to the scene, because deeper presence brings deeper impact. To read about starving children in Ethiopia moves us. To watch scenes depicting them on TV is even more moving, but to visit and actually see and hear the children firsthand has a much deeper impact. Similarly, reading Luke's account of Jesus healing the leper may stimulate thoughts and be a form of meditation, a discursive use of the intellect that leads to genuine prayer. If, however, I am able to be present to the scene by the use of the imagination, my heart may be intimately touched.

Time spent at the beginning of prayer in slowing down my racing mind, letting go of a busy agenda, disposing myself for the encounter and praying for help, helps me enter the scene. Ignatius proposes introductory steps called preludes. Some people begin to enter the stillness by doing awareness exercises, such as observing their breathing. Then they use the discursive imagination to make the scene fully alive and personal.

When I was teaching a Shakespearean play in a high-school class, there were several ways I could follow. The first way was to go through the text, concentrating on its meaning and explaining difficult passages. This was an intellectual study of the play, and was necessary if the genius of Shakespeare was to be opened up to the class. There was a big risk, of course, that the magic of Shakespeare would be lost and the play would just be seen as an intellectual exercise and lack appeal. This method was necessary, however, to introduce many students to the play, and roughly corresponds to discursive meditation.

After interpreting the text I found it helpful to let the class listen to a tape. This presentation brought the play alive as the students listened to the interpretation given by the actors and noted the interplay of the dialogue between the characters. It was a form of being present to the play just by hearing what the characters were saying. It corresponds to the discursive use of imagination in prayer.

A third way was for the class to see a good performance in which they would be able to both hear and to see, and their imagination would be nourished by the stage presentations, the sound effects, the backdrops and so on. This was a way of being present to the play not only aurally, but visually, seeing the characters and hearing their dialogue. But the students were still spectators.

The most rewarding method was for the class to become involved in a serious production of the play. I was fortunate enough to be teaching English at a school where there was a tradition of presenting drama that way. When the students were acting, they lost themselves in the play, and they became the different characters. The whole person was involved, thinking, seeing, hearing, doing, and the more they could enter into the parts, the richer was their understanding and their love of the play. No longer were they spectators.

I think something similar happens when we engage in a scriptural contemplation. It's possible to read the text of a scene in scripture and to think about it and to see what it means. That can be helpful; but the whole experience is really one of the mind only, for the most part. If I can enter into the scene by using my imagination and be with Jesus as he is healing the leper (Luke 5: 12–16), if I can be so present that I hear him say, 'Of course I want to', and I see the compassion in his eyes, and if I hear with my imagination the leper saying, 'Sir, if you want to, you can heal me!'; if I am able to see that ragged, sick man on his knees, present before the Lord; if in addition, I am able to see the fear in the faces of the disciples, then I am no longer just thinking about the scene or watching, I am involved.

At times I might find myself identifying with the leper, very conscious of the leprosy of my own sinfulness. I might experience the intense desire to be healed that the leper had, when he cried out 'Sir, if you want to, you can heal me!'. As I lose myself in the leper, the scene begins to become an encounter just between me and Jesus. If I am able to experience the compassion of Jesus, if I can see his deep concern for that leper, then it may well happen that I become more deeply convinced of his great concern for me.

The essential quality of scriptural contemplation is that I be really present in the scene. The contemplative moment comes when I have lost myself in the Lord and there is a deep encounter, a 'surprise discovery' between us. Scriptural contemplation can lead into very deep prayer, into the prayer of union, of loving regard, of totally non-conceptual contemplation.

From the experiences I have had in leading groups in scriptural contemplation, and also from listening to people describing their prayer experiences of contemplation, I see two very great advantages that result from this form of prayer.

The first is that Jesus becomes very personal to us. This is not unexpected; if I wish to know somebody more deeply, I must spend time in that person's company, and also that person must reveal himself or herself to me. A superficial account of where the person lives, or what he or she does for a living, will never lead to a deep personal relationship. When that person is prepared to reveal to me who he or she is, his or her hopes, fears, failures and successes, in an atmosphere of trust, knowing that I will accept him or her, we are entering into a true encounter in depth.

That is the experience that takes place in a scriptural contemplation. By looking on Jesus the author and finisher of my faith, by seeing what he does, listening to what he says, being in touch with his deepest feelings and walking with him through Israel, I come to know him more, to love him more, to follow him more closely.

Eamonn Bredin, in his book *Rediscovering Jesus*, decides to follow the same journey as the disciples in the way they came to know Jesus.[1] They saw him as a man first, then gradually were led into the realm of faith, to discover him and to accept him as God—something they could not do until after Pentecost. Our knowledge of Jesus Christ normally is the reverse of their experience: we come to accept him as God as we accept the dogmas of our faith, and we journey backwards to discover him as truly man. It seems that some people never really discover Jesus Christ as man. They see him as only apparently human. Yet the reality of the Incarnation is that Jesus Christ is truly God and truly man.

Scriptural contemplation enables us to enter into the reality of Jesus Christ being truly man as we contemplate him in his humanity. As we see him crying, angry, sad, disappointed, happy, frightened, we come to a deeper realisation that he is like us in all things save sin. It is that development of a personal relationship with Jesus that is a fruit of scriptural contemplation. St Teresa of Jesus speaks of the help she got in her journey of prayer by contemplating the humanity of Jesus.

The second advantage that comes to us from scriptural contemplation is that the Gospel scenes become relevant to our own lives. Many times I have heard people share how the call of Peter, in Luke's description, merged into their own situation. I recall scriptural dialogues in Marriage Encounter groups on the subject: 'How do I feel when Jesus takes my few loaves and few fish and feeds the multitude and has twelve baskets left over?'. That Galilean scene of nearly 2000 years ago is brought into their present life. The blind man asking to be healed, Mary seeking for the lost child, and so many other episodes strike chords in the actual experiences of the people who contemplate such scenes.

There are certain things that block our entry into a scripture scene.

The first is that we intellectualise. Our prayer becomes a head trip. We think about Jesus. We think about the scene. The mind is a good place in which to begin, but prayer must move from there to the heart, and in scriptural contemplation the prayer moves from the mind to the heart by using the imagination to be present to the scene. 'I lose my head and come to my senses', to quote Fritz Pearls. Scriptural contemplation is more than merely thinking about a scene or studying its meaning.

Secondly, we must avoid just being observers. As I found in teaching English plays, getting really involved in the play made for a deeper experience of the play's story. Therefore, it is important that I become a part of the scripture scene. I may, for example, be in the boat with Jesus and the disciples when the storm is at sea. I may be helping them to bail. I make use of my imagination to walk with Jesus as he is looking for the lost sheep, or perhaps I myself am the frightened lost sheep. If I am just an observer, I will be detached. When I am a participant, I have become part of the action and I may find that my role will change from day to day.

A third barrier can be my moralising. By this I mean preaching to myself or preaching to others. Sometimes in group sharings I have heard people describing their prayer in such a way that they are preaching to others. For example, 'We should show much more trust in Jesus'. Later, one may draw conclusions from the prayer experience that are going to affect one's way of living, but during the prayer itself I think it is better to be so lost in the scene that one does not preach to oneself or to others.

A fourth obstacle can be theorising, wondering what would happen if Jesus were to come on earth today, or theorising about the conditions in Jesus' time, the economic situation, the political atmosphere and so on. Sometimes we may be tempted to twist our prayer experience to support a pet theory of ours. These barriers hinder a loving encounter with the Lord. The goal of scriptural contemplation is to come to that moment when I am lost in Jesus.

Once I boarded a plane from Tasmania and a woman got on with a young baby. While she was fixing her seat, getting ready to sit down, I held the baby for her. After she was seated, I still held the baby, and it was then I noticed that the baby never took his eyes off his mother, and that the mother kept looking at the baby. For me that is contemplation; 'Lost, all lost in wonder, at the God thou art'. There were no words going on between mother and baby, just this looking. But each was very present to the other.

That is the essence of scriptural contemplation, being present to the Lord and letting the Lord be present to me, as the mother was present to the baby, and the baby to the mother. Such an experience of being present to the Lord brings about a slowing down of thinking and talking. This is important; as Teresa reminds us, prayer does not entail much talking or thinking, but much loving. As we keep looking at Jesus, he may lead us into contemplation in the strict sense—a union of faith without words, thoughts or images.

Reflections

Contemplating the Call of the Disciples.

Slowly read Luke 5: 1-11. If there is no-one to lead the group in prayer, it may help to read this exercise slowly into a tape recorder, pausing where indicated by the ellipses. Then you can play back the tape and concentrate fully on the exercise. You can also use this method when praying alone.

Begin by reflecting that you are in God's presence and he is present to you, he has spoken to you. Thank him for his presence and praise and worship him . . . Then ask him to teach you to pray, to guide and protect you . . .

Imagine you are standing on a slope overlooking the Sea of Galilee. It is a pleasant, sunny morning. Feel the warmth of the sun . . . Look at the calm waters reflecting the sunlight. Imagine the people streaming over the hillsides, converging on a spot near the water's edge . . .

Looking down, you see Jesus. He notices you and smiles a welcome as he recognises you . . . In imagination, see him coming to you, calling out your name. 'I have called you by name. You are mine.' . . . Then he gives you a hug and you allow yourself to feel the warmth of his greeting . . .

'Thank you for coming,' he says. 'I'm so glad you are here, as I want you to witness what is to happen.' And as you look at him, you are moved by his sincerity. 'I'm always happy when you are able to spend time with me. Come with me.' . . .

You follow him, pushing through the crowd as he leads the way . . .

The crowd is getting bigger and jostling Jesus to the edge of the water. He reaches out for your support as he stumbles. You relish the moment; so often you have leant on Him. Now he leans on you, needs your support . . .

Jesus says to you: 'Look, Simon Peter has a boat down there. Go and ask him if he will lend it to us.' . . . Forcing a passage through the crowd, you come to Simon Peter. 'Jesus wonders if you will lend him your boat,' you say . . .

You can see that Peter is very tired and that his nets are neatly stacked away . . . He looks at you, then at Jesus, who waves to him, nodding as though to verify your message. Then he looks down at his nets and you sense that this is a moment of decision. What answer will he give? . . . You wait . . . Jesus waits . . . God waits . . . Simon Peter gets up, says, 'yes' and tells you to step into the boat as he pushes it out—his first 'yes' to the call of Jesus. It has cost him, and yet he feels wanted. Everybody will know he is important to Jesus and has been able to support him . . .

With a few strokes he brings the boat around and Jesus steps in. As it rocks, you steady him . . . Sitting down, he looks out at the big crowd.

You look around at them. They have brought with them many different hopes, reasons, expectations . . . Some have come out of curiosity, some out of longing, some to be healed, some to judge for themselves about what they have heard.

You look at Jesus. What is he thinking as he looks out at that sea of faces? What is he feeling? . . .

You look at yourself as you sit in the boat with him. What will he say? What are your hopes, fears, expectations? How are you feeling? . . .

He begins talking about the Father's love . . . 'Love one another . . . Don't hate anybody. Love your enemies. Do good to them that hate you,' he says.

He is so challenging, calling them to launch out into the deep, to let go of their well-tried formulas, their securities, to walk on the sea of their fears . . . You reflect on challenges he presents to you . . . How free are you to let go? . . .

You watch the crowd going away. Jesus looks at you. 'Will you also go away?' he says . . . He says to Simon Peter, 'Launch out into the deep and let down your nets'. Peter is stunned . . . *At this time of day?* he thinks. *After a frustrating night? And me so tired? What will the people think of me? What sort of a fisherman is Peter to go out now?* Watching his face, you observe the struggle going on. Will he risk his reputation? To lend his boat was not so difficult, but to risk his reputation, to go out on a limb . . .

And Jesus is waiting for Peter—for you . . .

'Master, we worked hard all night long and caught nothing, but if you say so, I will let down the nets.' Simon Peter has said 'yes' a second time, and to a more difficult call.

As the boat moves out, you see the shore fading. You look at Jesus and see that he is looking at you. 'Will you also trust me and let go of your securities?'

Now the nets disappear over the side. They are being weighed down by the huge shoal of fish. The fish are splashing, shining silver in the sun, tearing the nets . . . 'Come out and help us!' calls Simon Peter to his companions . . . Soon two boats, heavily laden, struggle to the shore . . .

Simon Peter is overwhelmed: 'Leave me, Lord, I am a sinful man,' he says.

You watch Jesus lift him up and hold him. 'Simon, do not be afraid; from now on it is people you will catch.'

This is the third step, Peter. Your boat, your reputation, now your life. And again you say 'yes', and leave everything to follow Jesus.

You and Jesus are alone, and you talk to him and listen to him about whatever comes into your mind and heart, just as one friend talks to another.

* * *

Finish by playing 'The Galilee Song' from the tape by Frank Andersen, *Everything I Possess* (Chevalier Press, Kensington, NSW, Australia).

End the prayer by saying the 'Our Father'.

Notes

1. Eamonn Bredin, *Rediscovering Jesus,* Twenty-Third Publications, Mystic, Connecticut, 1986.

Reading List

Anthony de Mello, *Sadhana,* exercise 22, pp. 73–9.

Marilyn Morgan Helleberg, *Beyond TM*, Paulist Press, New York/Ramsay, 1980.

Margaret Hebblethwaite, *Finding God in All Things,* Collins Fount Paperbacks, London, 1987.

Eamonn Bredin, *Rediscovering Jesus,* Twenty-Third Publications, Mystic, Connecticut, 1986.

8.

Learning by Heart

My memories of school are happy ones. In particular I am grateful that we were frequently made to learn poems by heart. Often now lines I learnt then come back to me, from *My Country, The Australian Sunrise, Said Hanrahan, The Old Bush School* and many others. Later my horizons were widened as I was introduced to the English Romantics, Browning, Tennyson and Shakespeare.

Learning by heart is an interesting phrase. It seems to mean that by dint of repeating the words of a poem to the memory, the poem itself begins to take hold of the heart. Certainly that was true for me. From memory to understanding to heart was the journey.

Recently I was engaged in a weekend of contemplation and healing with a group of people. I was saying that the prayer must move from the head to the heart. A man asked me 'How do you move your prayer to your heart?' Rather glibly, I replied that *you* don't move the prayer to the heart, *God* does.

As far as it goes, that answer is correct, but it does not go far enough. Further reflection on the question and my answer leads me to see a parallel between learning by heart and praying by heart.

Spiritual writers, when teaching about prayer, speak of the three powers of the soul—memory, intellect and will. They tell us that praying engages all three, but culminates in the will uniting us to God. By will they meant what often today we call heart.

Prayer of the heart, or praying by heart, means that what we have recalled (memory) and what we have understood (intellect) have now taken possession of the heart to some degree. So we are moved to acts of love, praise, thanksgiving or affection. No longer are we just remembering, or thinking; now we are loving.

The *Spiritual Exercises* of St Ignatius Loyola present something of a course in prayer. Some of the concepts proposed there may help. Much use is made of reflection and discernment of one's prayer experiences, repeating the prayer, and slowing down to look and listen. This prayer pattern helps reveal feelings as well as thoughts, and praying by heart engages the feelings.

It helps, therefore, to repeat one's prayer. This repetition does not mean going through the prayer again to give a better performance. It means returning to those places in the prayer where I experienced God's love in a moving way, where the consolation I enjoyed revealed God's presence. I go back to the points at which the Lord was revealing himself and I remain there, dwelling in his love. It may be that a few words, such as 'Do not be afraid, I am with you', or some particular thought, encouraged and warmed my heart. So I return to allow the encounter to deepen, and to savour the experience. St Ignatius wrote: 'It is not much knowledge that fills and satisfies the soul, but the intimate understanding and relishing of the truth.'[1]

Tasting and seeing how sweet is the Lord, feeling the graced experience in one's deepest centre—these are the gifts we are seeking as we wait patiently on the Lord during prayers of repetition.

It is important to note also at what points in our prayer we run into frustration, anger, sadness, confusion, or discouragement, and to return to these points. We do not return because we are masochists, but because we wish to learn where these feelings come from. Listening to the feelings, and welcoming them as friends, we discover the unfree, unloving attitudes they reveal. With such enlightment we can ask the Lord for healing.

Once in my prayer on John 14: 12, I was jolted by the words: 'I tell you most solemnly, whoever believes in me will perform the same works as I do myself, he will perform even greater works because I am going to the Father.' I was puzzled, disturbed, angry. How could I do greater works than Jesus? It didn't make sense. I knew then that I had to keep returning to that passage until I discovered what message my angry feelings were bringing me about myself.

After some time, I began to realise that I was identifying 'works' with miracles. When I accepted that Jesus' work was to tell the story of the Father's love and to love all as the Father was loving, I came to accept that I was to be the visible Christ in the world, now that his physical presence was no longer here as it had been during his earthly life. I noted then that my anger and confusion left, and I saw that I was being challenged to a deeper faith. This in turn led me away from absorption in myself to praying to Jesus for this faith.

The experience had been a wall. Now it was a bridge, because, by returning to the passage, I had allowed myself to wait on the coming of the Lord. Truly this was a 'surprise discovery', an encounter.

My own experiences, and those shared with me by others, reveal so often that the feeling of discouragement in or after prayer tells us that we have lost our focus on Jesus. Like Peter, who was mesmerised by the wind and waves, we have taken our eyes off the Lord and so lost the contemplative moment. Returning to that moment and consciously looking on Jesus, we are caught up in his love.

No two people have an identical relationship with the Lord; loving is very personal. As we keep returning to the place where the Lord encountered us and we the Lord, the renewed intimate meetings lead us more deeply into a unique covenant relationship. 'To see thee more clearly, to love thee more dearly, to follow thee more nearly' is a constant refrain in the *Spiritual Exercises,* and the frequent repetitions focus on that petition. We tend then to build up our own private language with the Lord. A deeply personal relationship grows between us.

Reflection on one's prayer is a great help, and it becomes a prayer in itself as I ask the Holy Spirit to guide me. The aim is to explore more deeply the prayer experience I have had, so that I may discover what God is doing and where he is leading me. What he does in prayer is always more important than what I do. Although I need to know in what ways I may be resisting his call, or where I am heading off in a wrong direction, this review is much more than a reflection on how well I prayed. It is part of the continual searching for my God.

Such reflection is very enlightening if you discuss your prayer with another. We can gauge the importance Ignatius places on the review of prayer from the fact that during a retreat a quarter of an hour is suggested for reviewing an hour's prayer. This will not be the normal procedure for most of us outside of retreat. It does, however, help growth in prayerfulness if some time is given to this reflection.

If there is no time after the prayer, Herbie Alphonso SJ recommends spending the last few minutes of the prayer itself making this review. This will reveal where the Lord is leading. Is there unfinished business? Should I return to this same place tomorrow? Is there some aspect that is beckoning? Am I being shown a particular call within my overall vocation, that quality of loving with which the Lord is gifting me, and which will tend to dominate our relationship?

During the review I look at any ideas or thoughts that came to me during the prayer. I go deeper to discern my feelings, my mood and any change of mood or shift in direction. Do I have a sense of the Lord's presence, loving me, calling, challenging? Am I saying 'yes' or hesitating, resisting, rejecting?

As I am searching out these inner experiences I am ensuring that in my prayer I am using my heart as well as my mind. Where is the focus of my prayer—on the Lord, on myself, on difficulties, on others? Am I aware of shifting my focus? Have I tried to rush the prayer so that I can go and do something else, or have I been able to listen to the Lord and to stay where he is meeting me? Was I able to wait on his grace, his say-so, or did I become very busy and active, and try to make things happen? How did I feel when I came out of my prayer—happy, encouraged, disappointed, discouraged, resentful? What messages are my feelings giving me? Can I take them to the Lord, saying, for example, 'Lord, I am disappointed. Are you disappointed in me?'

As I reflect on my prayer, would I describe it as talking, thinking, listening, looking, being, worrying, struggling, wrestling or resting? Am I worn out, or refreshed? Was my prayer petition, sorrow, thanks, love or praise? Questions like these show how we can profitably reflect upon our prayer experience.

Some people are helped by keeping a prayer journal, in which they jot down notes on their prayer. Writing can help us articulate the experience and make it clearer, less woolly. Reading over the journal may help us discover the prayer pattern and rhythm that best suit us.

Influenced by the discipline of daily dialogue that Marriage Encounter taught me, I began to write my journal in the form of a letter each day to Jesus. Writing it in the morning and reflecting on the letter in the evening helped me relate my prayer with the day, and the day with the prayer.

Reflections

1. Consider the following accounts of prayer experiences. Before you read the observations given, you might find it helpful to note your own reactions.

   The prayer has been on Mary Magdalene going to the tomb to anoint Jesus (John 20: 1-3, 11-18).

   (a) I went with Mary to the tomb to anoint Jesus and found the tomb empty. When Mary ran to tell Peter and John I stayed behind. Then she came back with them and I watched the two apostles inspect the tomb. Later Jesus revealed himself to Mary and they seemed so happy together. I walked away as I did not want to intrude.

   Reflect on this account before reading further.

   Notice that the focus is on activity. The speaker is an observer and gives no indication of his or her feelings. There is nothing about relationships and no evidence of an encounter with God or Jesus. The speaker's not wanting to intrude is possibly significant.

   What advice would you give to the speaker to help in the prayer? Do you think he or she sees prayer as a performance or an encounter?

   (b) I felt happy going with Mary to the tomb, and I admired her fidelity. When she left I felt very lonely and afraid. It was good when she returned, and I rejoiced at the meeting between her and Jesus.

   Again pause for your own reflections.

   In this prayer the focus is mostly on Mary, who is a supporting figure. There is an awareness of feelings. The activity is that of an observer, not of a full participant in the scene. Any sign of a personal encounter with Jesus? What is implied about the speaker? Do you think there is a good understanding of feelings?

   What advice would you give to the speaker to help in his or her prayer?

   (c) I began to reflect upon the loneliness of Jesus as he was waiting for Mary. Surprised at his longing for Mary and me. When he saw us, I thrilled to see how Jesus smiled his welcome. He was so happy when I stayed with him when Mary left. I didn't feel any need for words as he seemed content to be with me, and I with him. The experience was surprising and joyful.

How do you see this prayer:?

Here the focus is clearly on Jesus and the relationship with him. There is much about feelings, those of Jesus and those of the speaker. Mention is made of surprises, too. What suggestions would you make as a follow-up to this prayer?

(d) Mary and I went to the tomb of Jesus while it was still dark. I was thinking of the times I have been in the dark and not knowing what to do, where to go. In particular it occurred to me that even now I don't know what to do about my job and the new offer that is facing me. So I prayed to the Lord for light to see what was best to do. When Mary failed to recognise Jesus, I felt sad because of the times I fail to see him in the people I meet and in the events that happen. Then it seemed he called me by name, as he did Mary, and that gave me strength. I stayed with this for some time. Gradually it dawned on me that we had come looking for a dead Christ and not the Risen Lord. I stayed for a long time reflecting that I don't have to be perfect, always doing exactly the right thing. As long as I love as best I can, Jesus is happy. I felt much encouragement.

What is your reaction to this account?

This prayer brings the Gospel scene into the person's real life. There is a turning to Jesus when discouragement begins to appear, in the speaker's praying for light; sadness at failing to recognise Jesus does not take over. The movement is away from being with Mary, to being with Jesus. The speaker's focus is on Jesus and the relationship with him. There is a revelation of self and also of Jesus in this encounter. And we note that there is no haste or sense of urgency. It is leisurely prayer that brings encouragement, and this indicates the presence of the Spirit.

2. Be Satisfied that God is God.

> Francis and Leo had the habit of long, silent walks through the countryside.
>
> One day as Francis was walking behind Leo through the woods, they came to the slopes of a ravine at the bottom of which rushed a mountain stream.

'Sister Water,' cried Francis, approaching the stream, 'your purity tells us of the innocence of God.'

Jumping from stone to stone, Leo had quickly crossed the stream; Francis followed him more slowly.

'There is something on your mind,' said Francis to him simply.

'If only we could be as pure,' answered Leo, 'we too could experience the marvellous joy and the boundless force of Sister Water.'

There was a deep longing in these words as Leo sadly contemplated the stream, which never ceased to rush forward in its glorious purity.

'Come,' said Francis, pulling him by the arm, and the two set off once again on their walk. After a short silence, Francis turned to Leo.

'Can you tell me, brother, wherein lies purity of heart?'

'It's having nothing with which to reproach oneself,' answered Leo, without hesitation.

'Now I know why you are sad,' said Francis, 'because we all have something with which to reproach ourselves.'

'Yes,' said Leo, 'that's why I despair of ever attaining true purity of heart.'

'Ah, brother Leo, believe me,' continued Francis, 'do not be so preoccupied with the purity of your own heart; turn your eyes to God, admire him, rejoice that he himself is All-Holy; give thanks to him for his own sake. That, my little brother, is purity of heart.

'And when you are thus turned towards God, do not turn back on yourself. Do not ask how you stand in God's sight. The sadness at not being perfect, the sadness of knowing you are a sinner, is a human feeling, a human sadness. You must raise your eyes higher, much higher; there is God, the immensity of God and his unalterable splendour. Such a heart is at the same time emptied of himself and overflowing with God. It is enough for him that God is God. In that itself the soul finds its peace and happiness, and God is then its only source of holiness.'[2]

Take time to reflect before reading on.

In this story we see the different responses made by Francis and Leo as they come upon the mountain stream. I have found this passage to be helpful to many people.

Francis is walking slowly; Leo is hastening. Walking slowly is important in prayer so that the prayer has time to move from the mind to the heart. To transform thinking into loving takes time. The experience needs to be deeply assimilated.

Sometimes I meet people who take for their prayer each morning the liturgical readings of the day. This becomes an automatic practice, and it may mean that the matter presented is not relevant to what is happening in their lives. Living and praying need to be integrated. Moreover, I may be moving away from the grace of meeting the Lord that was given me yesterday. It is good to go back to the places where we met the Lord, as we have just seen. Often we find he has not moved away.

Francis looks at the water and sees his God and is happy, so he lingers. Leo sees in the water not God, but his own picture. He falls into the trap of comparing himself with the water and is saddened. Comparisons hinder intimacy. Our enemy tries to get us to compare ourselves with others. 'If only I could pray like X. How fervent he/she is!' When we do this during our prayer, we have shifted focus. Often it means, too, that we have forgotten that prayer is a gift.

Through the skilful questioning of Francis, we discover that Leo's feeling of sadness is coming from his own wrong understanding of God. He is really meeting the God of the Hundred Per Cent, an unreal expectation of perfection from himself. His sadness comes from his failure to meet these demands, and so he is led into discouragement and despair.

Francis seeks to heal him by directing his gaze to a God who loves him, away from the God of the Hundred Per Cent who is disappointed in him. Being mesmerised by our sinfulness is a dangerous form of self-absorption and creates a wall. Awareness of sinfulness that leads us to God becomes a bridge that enables us to experience the mystery of God's forgiving love.

3. Here is another example:

> For prayer I prepared Psalm 63, which is all about thirsting for God. This is a theme that has been appealing to me for some time and this psalm is a favourite one for me. So I approached the prayer with eagerness and expectancy. But the prayer was a shambles. I was very distracted and nothing seemed to work. At times I found myself getting angry with God for letting me down, but I soon put a stop to that. After all I don't deserve his attention. I'm wondering if I am cut out for this prayer life you are talking about. Perhaps it would be better if I just read Barclay's book of prayers.

How do you react to this account?

Here we have a good example of self-fulfilling prophecy, deciding in advance what is to happen. This means we forget prayer is a gift: we must allow God to be free. Notice that the prayer is really the *experience* of thirsting for God who seems to be absent, instead of a prayer about it, which would be much deeper. The speaker's anger is suppressed instead of being shared with God, and so the opportunity for an honest disclosure of self to God is missed. Discouragement then follows. Notice that all this begins when the focus shifts from God to one's poor performance in the prayer.

We may sum up these thoughts on the review of prayer by returning to the earlier description of prayer. We *listen* to the experience and *learn* from it. So we are drawn to *love* God, self and others, and to *live* a life in harmony with the God we meet in our prayer. Now one's heart is in the prayer, and the prayer is in one's heart. Praying by heart is God's gift.

Notes

1. Louis J. Puhl SJ, *The Spiritual Exercises of St Ignatius,* Loyola University Press, Chicago, Illinois, p. 2.
2. Eloi Leclerc, *The Wisdom of a Pauper,* Franciscan Publications.

Reading List

Margaret T. Dwyer RSC, *Wake Up the Sun,* Desbooks, Thornbury, Victoria, 1988.

Henri J.M. Nouwen, *The Way of The Heart,* Ballantine Books, New York, 1983.

Russell M. Abata, *How to Develop A Better Self-Image,* Liguori Publications, Liguori, Missouri, 1980.

Russell M. Abata, *Unlocking the Doors of Your Heart,* Liguori Publications, Liguori, Missouri, 1984.

9.

The Healing of Life's Hurts

It is good to reflect often on one's journey with God, as was described in an earlier chapter. In doing so, we learn how God is continually calling us into intimacy with himself and others, presenting deeper relationships. The invitation to be in love with him is not a once only event, but an ongoing offering of growth. There is a second and a third call, or a call within a call, to borrow Herbie Alphonso's phrase.[1] We may discover that our prayer always seems to focus on one theme, one aspect of our relationship. Perhaps, too, a new ministry will begin to present itself.

After many years' teaching, I found myself led into Marriage Encounter, Charismatic Renewal, Tertianship, Ecumenism, and the Healing Ministry. In each case I noted my own surprise and my initial resistance.

The Song of Songs (2: 9,10) describes so well the Lord coming into my life and meeting a wall of resistance, fear and incredulity.

> See where he stands
> behind our wall
> He looks in at the window,
> he peers through the lattice.

My Beloved lifts up his voice,
he says to me,
'Come then my love,
my lovely one, come.'

Despite my opposition, God continued calling. Thus I was drawn into the Healing Ministry, for instance, in quite a roundabout way.

A mother had taken her retarded young daughter to Mary Rogers, an English lady who was visiting Australia and who was considered to have the gift of healing. Mary Rogers prayed over the child and recommended a blessing by a Catholic priest (Mary then was Anglican) because she thought the little girl was possessed. I was approached to perform an exorcism. I replied that I was happy to see the mother and the girl, but that I was not prepared to pray the Church's official liturgical prayer.

So I met them, prayed over the little girl and was not aware of any demonic powers. Since Mary had returned to England, I wrote to her to describe our meeting and asked why she thought the little girl was possessed. She replied that the child's behaviour was so extraordinary when she was praying for her, that she was sure of it. I dismissed the event from my mind, judging that Mary Rogers was misled.

When, however, Mary returned to Australia, again on a mission of healing, she asked to see me. A couple who had spoken to me highly of Mary Rogers, and who had impressed me, invited me to their home, where prayers for healing were being held. Reluctantly and sceptically I went. Here I met Mary Rogers, and immediately I was aware of what I can only describe as her inner strength and tranquillity. I watched as she prayed over many sick people individually. Later she invited me to join her in a big healing rally to be held the following Sunday evening. I thanked her and said I was sorry but I was too busy.

When the Sunday arrived I could not get out of my mind the thought that Mary Rogers had asked me to join her, and to bring a medal of St Ignatius Loyola! So eventually I decided I'd go if a car were free—but I knew quite well that no car would be available. However, surprise, surprise! a car became available. Before long I found myself at the church. Cautiously I opened the door and peered in, expecting to witness a hysterical crowd singing and screaming. True, the church was packed, but it was so peaceful and prayerful. Mary, with a small band of helpers, was in the sanctuary praying silently. It seemed safe, so I entered. Slowly I moved along a side aisle until I was near the front, clutching my medal of St Ignatius for safety. I asked a helper to give Mary the medal, but he kindly told me to take it to her. This I did, and she thanked me and asked me to pray with her over a young man.

I still recall vividly my fears and doubts as I tried to do that. Laying hands on his head seemed to be the most difficult thing I had ever done. When Mary left me alone with him, I felt so naked and helpless. The tension began to drain out of the man's face and he told me that he felt as though a great load had been lifted off him. I was confused, struggling with my unbelief, wondering where all this was leading me.

That was my entry into the healing ministry, which has now become an integral part of my priesthood, 'a call within a call'.

Since then I have noted the growth of the healing ministry in the Churches. Authors like Ruth Carter Stapleton, Francis McNutt, Agnes Stanford, the Lynn Brothers and others have given much guidance. So also has the Charismatic Renewal. It is no surprise that with the development of deeper prayer life and devotion to the Holy Spirit there should also be a rediscovery of this important part of the ministry of Jesus. His ministry was essentially a ministry of healing. When we journey with him through his public life as He is preaching the word of God, he is also healing.

We find four areas of healing in Jesus' ministry. He forgave sin. He freed people from the power of evil. He restored people to physical health and also brought deep inner peace. Because he handed these gifts on to his Church, we have the Sacrament of Reconciliation, the Anointing of the Sick, and the Eucharist as ways by which people may be set free and strengthened. But healing is not limited to the Sacraments.

In recent times, as the theology of healing has been explored, attention has been paid to the healing of memories and inner healing. It seems to me that previously healing was understood to mean only physical healing. Many were reluctant to pray for that because of a theology of suffering that seemed to ask of them to offer everything up, to be in union with Christ crucified. It is true that some seem to be called to enter deeply into the redemptive sufferings of Jesus, but it is equally true that we are to use ordinary means to preserve our health. So we visit doctors. Why not pray? Running ahead of one's grace is not wise, or holy.

Among the ways of exercising this ministry of healing in today's Churches are charismatic meetings with the prayer and the laying on of hands, monthly Masses where there is the anointing with the Sacrament of the Sick, weekend sessions of prayer for healing, and groups who come together to pray and to help one another with the laying on of hands.

For a number of years now Father Frank Maher and I have been part of just such a group that meets at Richmond, Victoria. We celebrate Mass and then in a quiet, reflective atmosphere we all pray with the laying on of hands for those who wish to be prayed for. This group has developed a deep atmosphere of prayer and support, so much so that I have heard people present for the first time express wonder at the way the atmosphere has helped them. It was the prayerful silence at Mary Rogers' rally that helped me initially.

What we have come to see through our experiences is the importance of what is called inner healing. Inner healing is wider than healing of memories, which concerns our sorrowful mysteries—the hurts, failures, rejections, disappointments, and guilt, the heavy baggage from the past which we carry around with us. It is important that these memories be healed. Inner healing does this, but it is also directed at present situations, relationships, and future fears, frustration and loneliness.

Jean-Pierre De Caussade SJ (1615–1751), in his *Abandonment to Divine Providence*, rests his spiritual teaching on living in the present. His phrase 'the sacrament of the present moment' sums that up. Dr Gerry Jampolsky (*Love is Letting Go of Fear, Goodbye to Guilt, Teach only Love*) also stresses that the only time we have is the present and that we should not allow the past or the future to have destructive power over us. For Jampolsky we are liberated by love as we are freed from unfree and unloving attitudes. So much, then, of inner healing is concerned with developing loving attitudes.

The teaching of both these men I have found very helpful in my acceptance of the mystery of healing. It is very much a mystery, just as love, sin, and God are all mysteries. It is important that we pray to live comfortably with mystery. Karl Raher has said that if we don't love mystery, we cannot love God because God is mystery.

At first my understanding of healing was very limited, and I associated it only with physical cures and miracles. I had thought it presumptuous to be asking God to work miracles, so I was quite suspicious of a ministry that seemed to take for granted that one should pray to God for healing.

When I taught, I was operating out of strength, knowledge of the subject, teaching experience and confidence, but in the healing ministry I come out of human weakness, with little medical skill or training, relying on my faith, which can seem very shallow when challenged this way. What I have found is that the people who come along with faith and trust and with concern for others begin to build up my faith and my trust in God.

Recently I was praying Psalm 46, 'God ever present in time of trouble'. I came to see that I had always prayed to the God of power to ask him to come with his magic wand and change the situation—my sickness, someone's cancer, another's blindness and so on. The focus was always on physical healing. Of course, I am not attacking that sort of prayer. But what I began to see is that God is more interested in changing me and changing others—helping us to grow, changing our attitudes, teaching us to find him ever present in time of trouble—than in changing situations.

Jesus prayed to his Father to take away the chalice, to change the situation, but the astonishing fact is that the Father did not do that. Instead, he did something better. He came to share the Passion so that Jesus was strong enough to move towards Calvary and Resurrection. Psalm 46 no longer speaks to me so much of the God of power as of the God of presence. It has opened up to me the deep meaning of compassion, which is shared helplessness, the helplessness that generates strong hope because it rests not on what is human, but on what is divine.

We are not talking here of stoical resignation, but of a Christian attitude of accepting weakness and finding the love of God there embracing me, as I embrace my God, ever present in time of trouble.

The people with whom I have prayed, and over, in the many groups for the healing of life's hurts, and for the loving, wounded community at Richmond have all deepened my acceptance of the mystery of healing and the part this ministry has in my own life.

Julian of Norwich describes so simply our God wrapping us round with his love:

> At the same time as I saw this corporeal sight, Our Lord showed me a spiritual sight of his familiar love. I saw that he is to us everything which is good and comforting for our help. He is our clothing, for he is that love which wraps and enfolds us, embraces us and guides us, surrounds us with his love which is so tender that he may never desert us and so in this sight I saw truly that he is everything which is good, as I understand.[2]

Recently I was conducting a prayer weekend for the healing of life's hurts through contemplation and fantasy, and I began by posing the question to the group, 'Have you the gift of healing?' Once my own response to that question would have been very guarded, because I would have seen it as asking whether I could heal people of physical sicknesses. In all honesty I would have had to say 'no'. But since healing is concerned more with the wholeness of the person than with the physical ailment,

I think it possible to give a wider answer to the question.

Healing, praying and loving all go hand in hand. They are the helping Trinity. Healing is loving. When you heal, you love; when you love, you heal; when you love another, you affirm, you nurture and you cherish. You are saying to the other: you are lovable and I am glad that you are. I rejoice in your existence. I am happy because you are you.

Healing means more than soothing a hurt, wiping away tears, removing the explicit hurt. True, these may be the exercise of it, but in its full richness it means loving and helping the other's growth to wholeness. All this is true of loving oneself and healing oneself. To heal is to love, to help oneself and the other grow to wholeness, to discover the true real self.

Thus, the answer to the question: 'Have you the gift of healing?' is: if you can love, you can heal; if you can accept love, you can be healed.

I like the definition that Ruth Carter Stapleton gives: 'Inner healing is a process of emotional reconstruction experienced under the guidance of the Holy Spirit'. Healing, then, is loving, and it is moving into the love of God in our lives.[3]

There are different ways of *healing through contemplation*, but basically it means finding God deep within. You find him in your own inner silence where he always dwells, because your inner silence is his country. 'And if the Spirit of him who raised Jesus from the dead is living within you, then he will give life.' (Romans 8: 11) Healing through contemplation means getting in touch with your own deep faith, hope and love, which is the spirit of God operating within you. Since you are made in the image and likeness of God, by looking deeply within, through his help, you can meet him face to face. For this we need the peace that Jesus promised, his kind of peace. This goes beyond psychological peace, which is good, of course, and which some techniques produce. Techniques are never prayer, and techniques lead into prayer only when there is an encounter with God.

Sometimes the psychological peace we experience is just an encounter with oneself, and unless one moves through that to meet God, there is no prayer. A number of writers these days do speak about meditation as a means of leading to wholeness. In her book *In the Stillness Conquer Fear* Pauline McKinnon describes how she was healed of her agoraphobia. Anthòny de Mello, in his well-known book, *Sadhana, the Way to God,* proposes ways to reach into stillness through awareness exercises. When we meet the deep spiritual stillness that goes beyond psychological peace, I think we are touching the power and love of our healing God.

In the groups that I conduct on the healing of life's hurts, we take a scene from scripture in which Jesus is healing, and by means of scriptural contemplation open ourselves up to his healing power. As we have seen earlier in this book, scriptural contemplation of the life of Jesus makes him more personal to us and shows how relevant the scenes of his life are to our own day-to-day experiences.

Marlene Halpin, Dominican nun, and Anthony de Mello, Jesuit priest, both praise *fantasy exercises* as ways of healing memories. The claims they make I have found verified in the many workshops I have conducted. Fantasy has a power of healing, of freeing us from hurts, even though we may not know how that happens. I think it is because in fantasy, we move out of our usual thought patterns and are freed from tension. This releases spontaneity, which is an experience of freedom, the joy of being ourselves, of being what we spontaneously want to be.

In the sharings that follow these fantasy exercises conducted in a group, there is also much laughter and freedom in talking about the experience. Anything that can produce such an effect is healing.

Healing through the laying on of hands draws upon the consolation and strength that is experienced through touch: a hug, a warmly grasped hand, a hand on the shoulder. All these often communicate love more powerfully than words can. Sometimes people speak of a dramatic release of tension through the laying on of hands.

Once, at the end of a Marriage Encounter Weekend, when saying goodbye to a couple, I laid my hands on the head of the husband, who was a non-Catholic, and said to him, 'Jesus loves you'. He told me afterwards that it was as though an electric shock went right through him, freeing him. Some months later, he became a Catholic and he attributed that grace as coming from the experience of the laying on of hands.

We all know that there are situations of deep sorrow when words are hopelessly inadequate. Then it is that holding another or being held is the only way compassion can be communicated.

In the workshops that I have attended and that I have helped give, *group support* enhances healing power, as we experience the truth of the Lord's promise, 'When two or three are gathered together in my name, I shall be present there with them'. It is important that we experience being loved by God and by others before we face our hurts.

We have in us the power to heal ourselves, but this power needs to be released because experiences can obscure it.

Time spent reflecting on God's love for us and experiencing the support of the group helps release that power. When I am conducting a weekend, I usually spend the first half reflecting upon the love of God poured into our hearts. In that way we are all able to release the power of the Spirit that we have received. Only when we are strong enough is it wise to face specific hurts. Rushing in too quickly is not advisable.

Conrad Baars speaks of the necessity of allowing ourselves time to feel our anger and our hurts.[4] Racing too quickly to apologise or to be healed before we have felt the pain deeply may often be unproductive. So not only is it necessary to have time to experience God's love, it is also necessary to have time to experience the pain of the hurt. When we are ready, we move into the healing of the hurts. The relationship of trust and love that has been built up in the group brings healing support.

I think it is unwise to pray over somebody for the healing of memories before a relationship of trust and love has been established. This also takes time. Emma Pearce says in her book, *The Pain of the Possible,* that we have the power to heal ourselves, but we need companionship to help us tap into that power.[5] Praying, loving and healing go hand in hand.

Just as there are barriers to listening and contemplation, there are barriers to the healing process. The first step is to break through the barrier of denial. We see this presented in the AA programme and the GROW programme. I must admit that I have a problem, that I need help. I need to acknowledge that I am hurting, that I am angry or that I am depressed.

The first step in our Eucharist is always to break through the barrier of denial after we have become aware of the presence of God: 'Lord I am a sinner, please have mercy on me.' Acknowledging my weakness, accepting my limitation, expressing my need of the Lord and affirming my confidence in his power to help me, are all part of the healing in every Eucharist. The word 'heal' is expressed explicitly just before receiving the Eucharist, but the whole experience of listening to the word of God and offering our gifts to him is just part of the movement back and forth to him which brings an increase in our faith, our hope and our love. One could say that the Eucharist is a dance of words and gifts.

Harriot Goldhor Lerner has written a book called *The Dance of Anger*, in which she explores most helpfully the movements taking place when anger has come into a relationship.[6]

It is very important in the acknowledging of one's anger or one's hurt to do so without blaming anybody, including oneself. As we say in Marriage Encounter, there should be no 'garbage dumping'. It is not always easy for us to accept that nobody hurts us without our permission and nobody makes us angry. By owning that I am angry, instead of saying, 'you make me angry', I move along the path to true freedom. True freedom implies accepting responsibility for my own life.

It is easy to fall into the trap of going back into the past and blaming parents, school, church and friends for where I am now. People love as best they can, and nobody except God loves perfectly. By laying on parents and on others the unreal expectation of perfect loving, we build up unreasonable resentment. Nurturing unreasonable resentment contradicts the loving that alone heals. By choosing life, not death, by accepting that forgiveness is at the heart of Christian loving, as the Lord's Prayer teaches, we are disposing ourselves both to heal and to be healed.

An unforgiving heart is the second big barrier to healing. As we break through this barrier, we move toward the mature wholeness of accepting responsibility for our own lives, instead of blaming others for our weaknesses and failures.

A Programme for the Healing of Life's Hurts

Very often when I am presenting a weekend for the healing of life's hurts, I follow a programme somewhat like this:

After an opening prayer invoking the power of the Spirit to guide, direct and heal us, I begin with a *Lectio Divina*—a reading—of the passage from Ephesians 3, verses 14-21. Elsewhere in this book, I have described the method followed for this form of prayer. Sharing the experiences we have is entirely voluntary, but usually I find that people are able to develop enough trust to reveal their experiences.

I next like to *explore prayerfully the image of God* that we have. As the Spirit leads us into a deeper awareness of God's unconditional, non-possessive, creative love, we are being disposed to face the hurts we have suffered. Sometimes I choose the fantasy exercise called 'The God Tree' given by Marlene Halpin in her book *Imagine That*.[7] At other times I am drawn to present the exercise given by Tony de Mello, which asks the group to go down to the city in search of God and then to imagine a symbol that best expresses God for them.[8] Fantasy exercises have the power to break open the deeper, hidden self. They also create a spontaneity that does much to relax and build up trust in the group.

We follow up this fantasy exercise with a *discussion* of the destructive images of God that may be influencing our relationship with him and with others.

Next follows a guided contemplation. Sometimes it is the call of Peter, as given in Luke 5, or it might be John's account of the call of the disciples in the first chapter of his Gospel.

Next I may introduce people to *mantra praying* and the *prayer of the Name*, so that the experience of meeting God goes deeper.

It is only after that preparation that we move into *the healing of hurts*. My favourite passage for this is a contemplation of the healing of the leper that is presented by Luke in chapter 5 of his Gospel. But sometimes I take the healing of the man at the pool given in John, or the healing of the man with the withered hand in Mark 3.

Following that, we have a *prayer of breathing*. Breathing in God's love, God's strength, and then breathing out one's hurts or sinfulness, or ingratitude.

I encourage people to *fantasise* about the joyful mysteries in their lives, to build up an album of love. When we are harbouring resentment, we are bringing from the past the deep feelings associated with the hurt received. Thus we are fantasising about our sorrowful mysteries. We can also do that with the joyful mysteries. So we go back to the joyful occasions in our lives, not just to remember them, but to fantasise about them, to make them real to us now, and to be aware of the feelings they evoke.

We are enjoying wholeness or healing when we are able to integrate the joyful mysteries and the sorrowful mysteries in our lives so that we enjoy the glorious mysteries. It is unreal to expect that one will go through life without being hurt. It is threatening to be afraid of life's hurts. The more love we bring into any situation, the more pain we are going to experience. For example, nobody on Calvary experienced the pain that Mary experienced, because nobody loved Jesus as deeply as she did. Loving makes us vulnerable. Being loved also makes us vulnerable.

In the intimacy of forgiving, when we allow back into a deep relationship the person who has hurt us, we become vulnerable because we have no certainty that it will not happen again. But loving in that forgiving way is learning to love the way God loves. He is continually allowing us back into the intimacy of a relationship with him, though he has no guarantee that we won't offend again. By reflecting upon the forgiveness that God gives us, we are able to enter into the mystery of unconditional loving.

We sometimes meet people who are able to forgive those who have hurt them deeply, even though they have no guarantee that the same injury will not happen again. Such people call us into the wholeness of loving unconditionally. They illustrate in their lives what Paul says in the first chapter of Colossians: 'You will have in you the power based on his own glorious strength, never to give in but to bear everything joyfully'.

Reflections

1. Have you had any experience of loving and healing another within the last few weeks? Recall the experience and then relive it. How were you led into that healing experience? Did you need to be freed so that you could reach out? How do you feel now as you recall the incident?

2. Have you any experience of being loved and healed? That is, of receiving a healing? How did it come about? Who took the initiative? Relive it in full detail. What are your feelings now as you recall that experience of being healed?

3. In her book *The Experience of Inner Healing,* Ruth Carter Stapleton gives many examples of taking Jesus back to a hurting experience so that the memories may be healed. Anthony de Mello also gives examples. The following exercise is based on what I learnt from his book *Sadhana*:

   Imagine Jesus being present to you in any way you wish. He says to you, 'I am the light of the world'. Then he lays his hands on your head. Imagine his healing light and strength moving into your mind and lighting up the dark areas of misunderstanding, critical judgments, remembered rejections, and so on. When in imagination you experience that light of love flowing through your mind, let it move into your heart to free you from the bitter resentment that has taken hold of your heart. Imagine that healing light helping you to let go of the idols that are enslaving you—especially the idol of an unforgiving, resentful attitude—and when you sense that light is freeing you from all the darkness, imagine Jesus saying to you, calling you by name, 'You are the light of the world'. Then recall somebody you wish to pray for and imagine that person being present with you. Spend some little time allowing that to happen, and then lay your hands on the head of that person. Imagine the love and light of Jesus flowing through you into that person's mind and heart.

After you have allowed yourself to experience the presence and love of Jesus so that your faith, your hope and your love are strengthened, go back with Jesus to the scene of the hurt. Imagine im walking with you and reconciling the two of you, looking at you and looking at the other person, saying to both of you, 'Love one another as I have loved you'. Linger lovingly.

Go to Calvary. Spend some time experiencing that scene and making it as vivid as you possibly can. Then go to the scene of your hurt and recapture it in detail. Be aware of your feelings. Then return to Calvary, allowing yourself to experience the pain of Calvary. Take plenty of time. Go back now to the scene of your hurt. Spend some time there, then go back to Calvary. Going back and forth, allow the love of Calvary to heal you.[9]

When hurts are deep and perhaps have been growing over time, they have been nourished by unfree, unloving attitudes. Normally, then, one should not expect instant healing. Healing is a process of growth and just as the unloving attitude has taken time to develop, so the loving attitude that will replace it requires time and prayer to soak in. Therefore, it may be necessary to continue praying in these ways persistently and confidently.

We know we are healing when we can recall the hurting experience and no longer feel the pain and the resentment, the anger and bitterness. When that happens, we thank God and keep praying for continued healing so that our freedom grows deeper and deeper. When we can even thank God for the experience and see all the good that has come out of it, we know we are healed. We have found Resurrection on our Calvary.

Notes

1. Quoted from Herbie Alphonso's workshop at Palmerston North Spirituality Centre, New Zealand, 1976.
2. Julian of Norwich, *Showings*, in Classics of Western Spirituality series, Paulist Press, New York, 1978, p. 183.
3. Ruth Carter Stapleton, *The Experience of Inner Healing*, Word Books, Waco, Texas, 1977, p. 9.
4. Conrad Baars MD, *Feeling and Healing Your Emotions*, Logos International, Plainfield, New Jersey, 1979.
5. Emma Pierce, *The Pain of the Possible*, P. E. Pierce, Gladesville, NSW, pp. 20–22.
6. Harriet Goldhor Lerner, *The Dance of Anger*, Perennial Library, Harper & Row, New York, 1986.
7. Marlene Halpin, *Imagine That*, William C. Brown, pp. 63–8.
8. Anthony de Mello, *Sadhana*, pp. 79–80.
9. ibid., pp. 82, 120.

Reading List

Agnes Sanford, *The Healing Gifts of the Spirit*, Trumpet Books, A. J. Holman Company, Nashville, Tennessee, 1976.

Francis MacNutt, *Healing*, Ave Maria Press, Notre Dame, Indiana, 1974.

Francis MacNutt, *The Power to Heal*, Ave Maria Press, Notre Dame, Indiana, 1977.

Matthew and Dennis Linn, *Deliverance Prayer*, Paulist Press, New York, 1981.

Ruth Carter Stapleton, *The Experience of Inner Healing*, Word Books, Waco, Texas, 1977.

Matthew and Dennis Linn and Sheila Fabricant, *Healing the Greatest Hurt*, Paulist Press, New York, 1985.

Matthew and Dennis Linn, *Healing Life's Hurts*, Paulist Press, New York, 1978.

Conrad W. Baars MD and Anna A. Terruwe MD, *Healing the Unaffirmed*, Alba House, New York, 1976.

10.

'Two or Three Gathered in My Name'

Group prayer may take many forms. Sometimes it may be silent reflection. At other times a group may be led into different ways of praying. This gives the opportunity for teaching, sharing and discerning.

I have been privileged to guide many groups in this way and have experienced the strength of group support, the presence of the Lord with the 'two or three gathered in my name'. Being part of a number of groups led by Anthony de Mello introduced me to the power of group prayer and to his method. Here I would like to describe some of my group prayer experiences.

A form of prayer I have found helpful for groups is the traditional prayer associated with the Benedictines, called *Lectio Divina*, the divine reading.

I take a passage such as Ephesians 3: 14–21, Paul's prayer. At the beginning we pause to slow down, to enter into silence, God's country, and seek to appreciate that we are listening to God speaking to us. His words are so precious that he has kept them alive in the scriptures, right up to this moment, so that we may hear them now.

After a short time of reflecting upon this, we offer a little prayer,

'Holy Spirit of God, source of all wisdom and truth, open our minds and our hearts that we may hear your word and keep it. We make this prayer through Christ Our Lord.'

Next I read the passage slowly and deliberately, right through to the end. After a pause for reflection, I invite any member of the group, who so wishes, to share with us any word, or any phrase that struck him or her. We are not looking for any comment on the word or the phrase, simply the word or phrase itself. Usually quite a number will mention a word or phrase, and there is a great variety in what appeals to the group. It is important to be aware of this, and to accept that the Spirit deals with each person individually.

Again I read the passage through, slowly and deliberately, to the end. After a pause I again invite anyone to share a thought or a feeling experienced during the reading. In other words, we are looking to see what the passage is saying to us, and how we are responding. Again there is a variety of responses. I take the occasion to reflect aloud with the person on the experience shared with us. Somebody might say that he or she was impressed by the phrase, 'May he give you the power through his Spirit'. That made the person think that the Spirit was with him or her.

I ask that member of the group to reflect upon the feeling that may be underlying the thought. Some people need to be helped in the journey from the prayer of the head to the prayer of the heart so that they become more alert to the emotional responses they experience as well as to the thoughts they are having on the word of God. It may happen that the person will say: 'I have a feeling of confidence', or 'I feel excited', or 'I feel strengthened in my trust of God from knowing the Spirit is with me'. I would then advise searching for other passages in scripture that would nourish that response to the word of God. If, for example, somebody felt that he or she had a sense of confidence in God's presence, I would suggest passages such as Romans 8, or the phrase from John, 'Have confidence, I have overcome the world'.

The purpose of this discerning of the prayer experience, and the reflection upon it, is to help members discover their own personal relationships with Jesus. Furthermore, becoming more alert to emotional responses as well as to the thoughts the passage arouses leads the prayer deeper into the heart.

This second round of sharings may take quite some time. That is of no concern, really, because it becomes a time of enlightenment for all members of the group as they listen to the experiences of different people. It is important to emphasise that there is no such thing as a right experience or a wrong experience. Very often, the so-called disappointing response turns out to be extremely helpful. I also stress that comparisons between experiences is not helpful at all. Such comparisons can destroy the intimacy of the personal relationship that God is building up with each member of the group.

I now read the passage for the third and the final time. After some reflective silence, I then invite people to share with us a prayer that arises out of their experiences of that passage. Once again, there is a variety of prayerful responses. Someone may pray in thanksgiving for the presence of Christ in the heart. One may pray a prayer of petition for deeper faith. Another may pray for the hidden self to grow stronger, and so on. Spontaneous prayer comes from the heart responding to the word of God, and is the authentic answer of the true self.

At the conclusion of that prayerful exercise, I describe more fully the *Lectio Divina* prayer. Normally I prefer to have the group go through an experience before explaining more deeply the form of prayer we have been using. There are three elements, or stages, in the *Lectio Divina.* The first stage is the reading, the *Lectio.* Here, one is just listening to the word of God. In a group situation the reading continues to the end. I point out that when doing this prayer on one's own, one stops whenever a word or phrase begins to appeal. There is no need to go through the whole of the passage. But since the group situation is partly teaching through the prayer experience, and since there are a variety of responses in the group to that passage, one reads through to the end. When reading alone, it is usually best to read aloud, if that is possible.

The second stage is the *Meditatio,* as it's called—the meditating. This means reflecting on the phrase that has most appealed. I turn over in my mind the word or phrase I have chosen. For example, I may be struck by 'my hidden self grow strong', and I turn this over and over reflectively, saying 'my hidden self grow strong', 'hidden self grow strong', and sometimes I might wonder why I am hiding, or what the self is that is hiding, or what it means for that hidden self to grow strong. Ruminating in this way, I begin to allow the passage to unfold itself to me.

It is not enough, however, just to be aware of how I am responding intellectually to the word of God. I also need to know my emotional responses. The phrase, 'hidden self grow strong', may fill me with a deep desire for the Spirit to do this in me. It may also arouse fear of what will happen. Whatever the response is, it is important to discover it, because until a thought takes hold of the heart, there will be little effect upon one's behaviour.

As I am ruminating on the phrase, there is space and time for the feelings to surface. All this is part of the meditating. It may happen, and often does happen, that the meditating slows down, and one moves into a stillness that we can call contemplating—just resting in a word or a phrase. A sort of stillness, peacefulness or contentment takes hold of one. When that happens, it is important to remain thus, relishing the truth that is taking hold of the mind and heart. One remains as long as the soul is relishing the truth.

The third stage is called *Oratio,* prayer. Everything in the *Lectio Divina* is directed towards the encounter with God which we call prayer. The prayer may be expressed with spontaneous words or without words, just resting in the experience of God touching the soul. This experience is, of course, personal, and is the reaction one *has* and not the reaction one *should have.* Once again, we see the importance of being true to one's own response to the word of God.

These three stages, reading, meditating and praying, are descriptive, not prescriptive. Sometimes one is carried almost instantaneously into responding to God as we hear or read the words.

This form of prayer is a very simple but deep way of praying the scriptures. It is a way of allowing the prayer to move from the mind to the heart and can be a gateway to deeper contemplation. The scriptures provide very rich material for this sort of prayer, but it need not be confined to scriptures. One also may take the prayers of the Mass or well-known prayers such as the Hail Mary or the Our Father, and by saying these slowly and reflectively discover that they have a personal significance and enrich one's relationship with God.

When I am leading a group, praying the passage from Ephesians called Paul's prayer, I suggest that members might like, at times, to adopt something that I have found helpful. I explain I am seeing it not as Paul's prayer, but as Jesus' prayer for me. I spend a little time becoming aware of Jesus' presence, of him telling me he is praying for me the way Paul told the Ephesians he was praying for them. When I am sufficiently aware of the presence of the Lord Jesus, I read the passage aloud as though Jesus were saying it to me. It goes this way:

> Frank, this then is what I pray, kneeling before the Father from whom every family, whether spiritual or natural, takes it name. Frank, out of his infinite glory, may he give you the power through his Spirit for your hidden self to grow strong so that I, Jesus, may live in your

> heart through faith. Then, planted in love and built on love, you will with all the saints have strength to grasp the breadth and the length, the height and the depth, until knowing my love which is beyond all knowledge, you are filled with the utter fullness of God.

This can help me to become more aware of Jesus forever interceding for me at the right hand of the Father.

I have found the experience of the *Lectio Divina* a helpful way of introducing a group to prayer and to searching for the emotions. In the reflections that are made on the responses they share, the group can be introduced also into the practice of discerning individual prayers and discovering the journey the Spirit wishes to take each person on. It seems also non-threatening to begin the group's sharings by asking just for a word or a phrase that struck them, without asking for the accompanying thoughts and feelings.

The spiritual direction given in this group experience often is a good introduction to individual spiritual direction, and a helpful preparation for an individually directed retreat.

Reflections

Praying with your breathing and your eyes moves the prayer out of the head to the heart. A great enemy to prayer is tension, so these simple methods are very relaxing. Moreover they encourage affectionate prayer, which in turn may lead into contemplation

1. Breathing Prayer— 'Breathe on me, O breath of God'
   Spend time entering into stillness, in a very leisurely manner, with no haste or urgency. Just wait patiently with expectation for the coming of the Lord.

   Be aware of your breathing—breathing in, breathing out.

   If your mind is racing, don't worry. Don't fight the distractions. If you do, they will fight back. Don't blame or punish yourself. Be aware of your distractions, of the workings of your wonderful mind. 'Thank you, God, for this beautiful mind.' Return gently to observing your breathing in, breathing out.

   Gradually accept that you are surrounded with air, and that you need air for life. Without air you will die. As you breathe in, you are breathing in God's life-giving gift. God comes in, with his gift. You are breathing in God's love, his life, his strength.

You are breathing in God. Allow his healing power to go deeply into your heart. Allow the light of God to break through into those dark, hidden places, where fear, hurts and resentment are buried. Allow the breath of God to free you, to push open the gates of these prisons.

As you breathe out, let go of the fear, the hurts, the resentments.

Breathe in God, breathe out your false self. Breathe out thanks, praise, sorrow, love.

Breathe in God.

Breath out yourself in full surrender to his love.

2. Prayer of the name—'I have called you by name, you are mine'
Spend time entering the stillness. Imagine Jesus calling you by name. Listen to his tone of voice. How does he speak your name? In your imagination, keep listening to Jesus calling you by name.

'You are mine, I have called you by name.'

Begin calling Jesus by name. How do you pronounce it? What do you communicate? Keep saying the name of Jesus in a gentle rhythmic way.

'I have called you by name, Jesus, you are mine.'

The Jesus prayer tends to begin on the lips, move to the mind, and then into the heart, as we continue the rhythm.

Keep repeating the name of Jesus and your own name, alternating between the two.

3. Prayer of the eyes—'Looking on Jesus, the Author of our Faith'
The eyes are a powerful means for communicating. Jesus looked hard at the disciples when they were following him, sadly at the rich young man and at Peter in the courtyard.

Look on your crucifix and through your eyes look on Jesus with praise, or hope, or love, or sorrow, or however you wish.

Imagine Jesus looking at you from his Cross. What are his eyes saying?

Make a visit to the Blessed Sacrament and gaze attentively at the tabernacle. What do you wish to say with your eyes? Stay, quietly expressing the sentiments in your heart.

Imagine Jesus looking back at you. What is he telling you? Relish it deeply.

Reading List

Per-Olof Sjögren, *The Jesus Prayer,* SPCK, London, 1975.
R. M. French, *The Way of the Pilgrim,* SPCK, London, 1972.
Tom O'Hara SJ, *At Home With the Spirit,* Jesuit Publications, Richmond, Victoria, 1989.
John Main OSB, *Word Into Silence,* Darton, Longman & Todd, London, 1980.
Mark Link SJ, *You,* Argus Communications, Illinois, 1976.
Archbishop Anthony Bloom, *Living Prayer,* Darton, Longman & Todd, London, 1966.
Merlin Carothers, *Prison to Praise,* Hodder & Stoughton, London, 1972.
Mark Link SJ, *Breakaway,* Argus Communications, Allen, Texas, 1980.

11.

Praying Together as a Couple

Since Vatican II there has been a remarkable outpouring of the Spirit on the Church and the world. Signs of it are the growing hunger for prayer, the gradual healing of the scandal of division in the Body of Christ, the rediscovery of the ministry of healing, the growing understanding by the Church of matrimonial spirituality. Teams of Our Lady, Marriage Encounter, the Catholic Family Movement, Christian Life Communities and the Retorno movement are some of the signs of this vitality in the Church.

Here I wish to write about Retorno, because this experience is filling a gap in the prayer life of the Church. We have directed retreats by which people as individuals go to God, retreats for different groups in their journey to God, public liturgy to provide for the community, but little to help the couple go to God together as a couple.

The Retorno was first offered in Spain in 1970. Father Gabriel Calvo, the founder of Marriage Encounter, found that encountered couples, who had achieved a deeper relationship with each other, came to him seeking help because, they said, they were now hungering for a deeper relationship as a couple with God. So the Retorno Weekend grew out of Marriage

Encounter. It is really a deeper entry into the 'Us and God' phase of the weekend, and in a less intense programme helps couples to develop their prayer as a couple. The presentation focuses on Father, Son and Holy Spirit, and the couple pray about the will of the Father, the Gospel of Jesus, and their witness to love and unity in the Spirit.

I have found this to be a deep experience in my own prayer life, and seen its influence in deepening the matrimonial spirituality of the couple. The movement into the Trinity seems to parallel what happens with the prayer of many of the mystics. In fact, there is a deep mysticism in marriage, and husband and wife praying together open each other up to this great gift.

At first many couples are afraid of sharing their inner spirituality. This reluctance may be due to the fact that it is quite a new experience to them. Yet as they develop deeper sharings of other aspects of their life together, they will be more confident about entrusting their spiritual inner life to each other. Sometimes there is fear caused by diffidence about their relationship with God, an attitude that 'Surely what I am experiencing is not worth listening to'. Many religious and priests making their first directed retreat can relate to that fear; they have had to overcome it. But 'Love is letting go of fear'.

Again, it is not easy to put into words your inner experiences. How difficult it can be for couples at the beginning of their Marriage Encounter Weekend to discover their feelings and then to express them! This they learn to do just by trying, and by the encouragement given and received. The same holds for sharing your prayer life with the one you are sharing your life with. Letting go of a 'married singles' way of life leads couples into the power of living as a married couple. The Retorno Weekend extends this new way of living into a new way of praying, that is, praying not as two people who happen to be married, but united, as a married couple.

At times I have spoken to couples who expect that because of their deep closeness they should have similar prayer experiences. This, I think, is a wrong expectation. God treats each one of us as a separate person. Even when he gives us the gift of close union with him, our personalities remain differentiated. This is true also when husband and wife are very close. Each person is unique. In my spiritual direction of married couples, I find it important to remind them not to have unreal expectations. By sharing with each other their individual personal experiences they are enriching each other. God does not clone, and the Spirit's gifts are most varied.

I remember a couple who were making a live-out retreat, known as the 19th Annotation Retreat. They were going through the *Spiritual Exercises* over a period of thirty weeks. Once a week each would see the spiritual director and talk things over with him. The husband was surprised and disappointed that, while his wife was enjoying spiritual consolation, he was struggling with spiritual desolation. From that they both learned that no matter how close their relationship was, they could have very different experiences. God cares for each personally.

There are a number of ways of praying together as a couple. One is suggested by Father Armand Nigro SJ in a leaflet handed out on a Retorno Weekend.

1. While sitting together or lying in bed together, feeling each other's closeness, take time in silence to be aware of God's presence.
2. Listen together to a short passage from the living word of God in the Bible, while one reads it aloud slowly. Then, pause and let the words silently sink in for a couple of minutes.
3. Say to each other as briefly as possible what God's words mean to you. Then, more silence.
4. Finish by speaking directly to God the Father and to Jesus and to their Spirit, even if it is only, 'Thank you, Lord. Stay with us.' Speak out to the Lord your faith and hope and love, your longings and complaints and gratitude, your joy and praise and adoration, your sorrows and disappointments and whatever moods and feelings are yours.
5. Repeat the above four steps two or more times.

It could take ten minutes or longer, according to the needs and moods of each couple. The important thing is to consciously, simply and honestly share aloud one's relationship to Father, Son and Holy Spirit.

Isn't it strange, even tragic, that so few Christian couples do this? They share meals and conversation, work and play; they share their own bodies and hopes and plans, but they do not openly share Jesus together. Yet Jesus is their deepest reality, their deepest source of unity, joy and fulfilment.

What can I say to couples who might read this chapter, except 'Try it! You'll like it!' It can transform a couple's life and fill it with joy and beauty. It can be really a taste of what Heaven is.

Another method is Scripture Dialogue. Select a passage from scripture that describes a scene and that means something to you as a couple. One of you read it slowly and aloud. Whichever partner is more imaginative should then set the scene, making it as vivid as possible. Do this slowly. Re-read the passage slowly. Then write a letter to your partner describing the thoughts and feelings you have as you reflect on Jesus speaking to you as a couple. Next, exchange your letters to learn of each other's reactions. Discussion could follow.

Another way is for each to write a letter to Jesus expressing his or her responses to the passage. Then husband and wife exchange their letters.

Perhaps there is no time for writing. If so, share with one another the thoughts and feelings aroused in you by the passage, after the second reading.

When couples become comfortable with going to God together, they can experiment with different ways of praying to find their own suitable rhythm. I have met couples who are accustomed to praying separately by meditation or contemplation and later to sharing their prayer with each other.

Reflections

1. Imagine Jesus saying to you as a couple 'Love one another as I have loved you'. Ponder prayerfully on these words. Be aware of any thoughts and feelings they cause to arise in you. Share these with each other.

2. Hear Jesus say to you as a couple: 'I am the vine, you are the branches'. Prayerfully ponder on these words, and share your thoughts and feelings about them.

3. Some scriptural scenes to imagine:
   Luke 7: 1–10
   Luke 7: 11–17
   Mark 4: 45–56
   John 1: 35–51

4. Some scriptural passages to read and meditate on:
   Ephesians 3: 14–21
   Romans 8
   Colossians 1: 10–14.

5. Let one partner slowly read aloud Paul's description of love in 1 Corinthians 13: 4–13. Then look into one another's eyes and ask each other for healing forgiveness for any failures.

6. Say the Rosary together, explicitly coming to God not as two individuals praying together, but as one couple united in love.

7. Father Louis Savary SJ has coined the word 'kything' to describe the new spirituality of the couple. Kything is the 'Act of being spiritually present to each other'. While as individuals we are called to join our hearts and souls to God, in matrimonial spirituality there is a further step. Your deep couple centre, the fruit of your loving union, is called to a loving union with God. Discuss this with one another, and with other couples.

8. The Church has called your family 'the little Church', and speaks of your relationship as a couple as a mirror of the Trinity. Share with each other your thoughts and feelings about these images.

Reading List

Tom and Lyn Scheuring, *God Longs for Family*, Our Sunday Visitor, Huntington, Indiana, 1980.

Tom and Lyn Scheuring, *Two for Joy*, Our Sunday Visitor, Huntington, Indiana.

Joan Meyer Anzia and Mary G. Durkin, *Marital Intimacy*, Loyola University Press, Chicago, Illinois, 1980.

Paul Tournier, *To Understand Each Other*, John Knox Press, Atlanta, Georgia, 1967.

John Powell, *Why Am I Afraid to Tell You Who I Am?, Why Am I Afraid to Love?, The Christian Vision*, Argus Communications, Allen, Texas.

12.

Passionate Encounter with a Passionate God

There is a continuing interest in mysticism. The shelves of recent books on prayer carry the writings of Julian of Norwich, Hildegard of Bingen, Catherine of Siena, Thomas Merton, and many more. Writers like Anthony de Mello, George A. Maloney, William Johnston and Matthew Fox are just some of those who are in demand. Many Christians, especially among the young, are attracted to Zen Buddhism, to Hindu Yoga, to occultism, to the ashrams of India in their search for a direct experience of God. It is sad that often Christians are unaware of the rich treasury of mysticism in our own Western tradition.

Often there is confusion about the meaning of mysticism nowadays. The word is sometimes used to mean demonology, witchcraft, the occult or psychic phenomena. Or it may be applied to somebody who is a dreamer, out of touch with reality. A poet such as Wordsworth can be labelled mystical because of his love of nature, and poets, painters and musicians who have deep visions are often said to be mystical. This varying use of the term creates much ambiguity and even suspicion. Let me try to clarify the meaning given to mysticism in this book.

George A. Maloney SJ, in *The Breath of the Mystic,* writes: 'Mysticism is a living experience of God, not as an object outside of us, but as an encompassing power of permeating love that, as St Augustine said, is more intimate to me than I to myself.'[1] It is an authentic encounter with the God within; it is being caught up in the Holy Spirit breathing within me; it is absorption in the dialogue between the Christ who lives in my heart through Faith and Abba Father. Mysticism means union with a loving God.

Experiences with spiritualism, demonology or witchcraft, are not God-directed and so are not included in our understanding of mysticism. The artist's insights may be the door leading into union with God—so often beauty does this—but unless the encounter with God takes place, there is no mysticism.

We are here considering Christian mysticism, the loving union that flowers forth from the scriptures and Jesus Christ. The East has its own great tradition and the exchange between East and West is most enriching. Here, however, we confine ourselves to the West.

I propose looking at three different expressions of Christian mysticism. First of all there was mysticism understood in a strict sense. Then, in recent times, it has come to be understood in a wider sense. Finally, there is the growing understanding of the invitation to unite with Jesus in the paschal mystery. I present examples of mystics who represent these three different expressions to aid in the understanding of our rich Catholic spirituality. I hope that ultimately we may come to see that all Christians are called to the mystical life, and that the essence of Christianity is mysticism.

Mysticism in the Strict Sense

The term 'mysticism' is of relatively recent origin. During the medieval period, 'contemplation' was the more popular term. But before that, or at least from the sixth century onward, theologians preferred the expression 'mystical theology'.[2] So we don't find the term in John of the Cross or Teresa of Jesus, yet both write about contemplation.

The distinction is made between *acquired* contemplation and *infused* contemplation. Acquired contemplation is prayer we work at with and through grace. Teresa describes stages of prayer in *The Interior Castle*, calling them 'mansions', and the first three mansions concern the ordinary prayer that reaches its highest level in acquired contemplation. John of the Cross spells out the signs that reveal a call to move on into infused contemplation.

Infused contemplation is known as mystical understanding, also called mystical wisdom and mystical theology. It is called 'mystical' because it is secret or hidden knowledge. It is called infused because it is not gained by the work of the intellect, the imagination, or the senses, but freely poured into the soul by God. This knowledge gives rise to love and to union. The last four mansions of Teresa's Interior Castle deal with infused contemplation. Ignatius speaks of 'consolation without preceding cause' and this may be infused contemplation.

In the Western tradition some mystics follow the dark, hidden road that is called the *via negativa,* the way of negation, the apophatic way. This means they are led into infused contemplation without using words, concepts or images in their prayer. The senses, the imagination and the intellect are, as it were, blacked out. Their prayer is non-conceptual, imageless. It is the dark road of faith. Chapter 14 of this book, 'The Cloud of Unknowing', describes this form of prayer. St John of the Cross is classified as an apophatic mystic.

But we also find mystics like St Teresa of Jesus, and St Ignatius Loyola, who follow what is called the affirmative way. They use images and concepts in their prayer. They are called kataphatic mystics. It is to be noted that both the negative way and the affirmative way move toward passionate union with God.

All this terminology tends to make prayer and mysticism complicated, and may prove a barrier to understanding it.

There is another difficulty that many have. When we think of mysticism we think of all kinds of psychic phenomena—visions, locutions, stigmata, ecstasy, trances. It should be clearly understood that psychic phenomena do not constitute mysticism, although they may be produced in various ways and may at times accompany mysticism. Nevertheless it is only the direct encounter with God that causes the purifying, illuminating, transforming union of love which is the essence of mysticism. This is God's free gift of grace.

Some may be trapped by pseudo-mysticism. Certain methods of relaxation can be very helpful for producing peace, but if I am seeking peace for its own sake, my journey inwards is narcissistic, concerned only with myself. Unless there is an encounter with God, unless I am seeking the God of peace, and not merely the peace of God, there can be no prayer. True, these exercises may prepare us for deep prayer and so can be helpful, but let us not call them mysticism. The essence of mysticism is the living experience of God.

Mysticism in the Wider Sense

In recent times, writers like Karl Rahner, Hans Urs von Balthazar, Thomas Merton, William Johnston and Anthony de Mello have described mysticism more broadly. They see it as part of the everyday life of the committed Christian. It is the experience of the holy, loving presence of God. At times there may be an explicit awareness of God in our lives; at other times he is felt implicitly, vaguely.

Thomas Merton believes all Christians are called to the mystical life. Those who are aware of their experience of God loving them are explicit contemplatives. But there are 'masked' contemplatives who have the experience without being conscious of it. Harvey Egan comments: 'Merton seems to be in agreement with Rahner and other contemporary commentators who speak about mysticism as a deepened form of ordinary human experience.'[3]

Many modern writers avoid the distinction between infused and acquired contemplation, viewing it unhelpful. Abbot Butler says that these two forms of contemplation differ not in kind but in degree. It has always seemed to me that the distinction between a grace that is extraordinary (infused) and one that is ordinary (acquired) is arbitrary. Surely all grace is extraordinary.

This modern approach is opening up the richness of deep mystical prayer for many. It is seen not as something reserved for the privileged few, the great saints, but for all who believe in and follow Jesus Christ. Their innate yearning for God is leading them into an intimacy with Jesus as they leave themselves open to the guidance of the Holy Spirit. So I meet many mystics in this wider sense at retreats, at charismatic prayer groups, and in my Marriage Encounter apostolate.

Union with Jesus in the Paschal Mystery

When some Greeks said they would like to see Jesus, he replied that the seed must fall into the ground and die for new life to be born (John 12: 20–32). He was referring to his own Passion, Death and Resurrection and inviting his followers to unite with him in the paschal mystery. So, too, when Peter made his great profession of faith in Jesus, 'You are the Christ', there was the same invitation into an intimate following of a suffering, dying, rising Jesus. Simon Peter was not yet ready and he drew back. Later he would accept this call to intimacy, but only after he had been born anew at Pentecost (Matthew 16: 13-28).

There are many who give themselves generously to following Jesus, as in their sufferings they find the God who loves them into new life. Etty Hillesum, in the concentration camp at Westerbork, cried with joy at God's love for her. Instead of asking why this was happening to her, she tried to comfort God 'who is so helpless'.

Joni Eareckson, crippled after a diving accident, discovered that her wheelchair was her cross and her pulpit. Just as Jesus, when lifted up, drew all to himself, so his modern disciple is drawing many to him as her journeying into the paschal mystery is revealed. Because of her paralysis, Joni has come to exercise a fruitful ministry of preaching and writing.

Corrie ten Boom, Simone Weil, Maximilian Kolbe and all the modern martyrs, the countless men, women and children who are uniting their sufferings with the sufferings of Jesus, are all mystics, it seems to me. They find God in the midst of their pain, just as Jesus did in Gethsemane.

My own involvement in the Healing Ministry has opened me up to the power and glory of the Cross in the lives of the sick. Many years ago, when working as a chaplain in the hospital at Flushing, New York, the sick revealed to me the mysticism in their lives. Through them I learned that God's love is at the heart of sickness and dying. In later years, the experiences with healing groups, especially our community at Richmond, have deepened this awareness.

Mystics walking with Jesus in his paschal mystery are God's gift to the Church and the world.

Reflections

1. What do you understand the paschal mystery to mean? Holy Week? The Eucharist? Suffering? All three?

   Reflect on any experience in your life that was calling you to enter the paschal mystery. Did you recognise the invitation at the time? How did you respond?

2. Do you know of anyone whose life of suffering seems to be an inspiring one? What is there about this person that inspires you? Do you know someone whose suffering seemed to be destroying them? What do you think is the cause?

3. Etty Hillesum experienced the God of love in the concentration camp. Joni Eareckson was led eventually to discover God's blessings in her accident, by her friend reminding her that for those who love God all things work for good. Do their experiences speak to any area in your life? What transformed their sufferings?

4. In time of suffering, do you pray to the God of the magic wand or the God ever present in time of trouble? Refer to chapter 2, 'Second-hand Gods for Sale'. Does suffering make you bitter or loving, angry and full of self-pity, or compassionate?

5. Can you recall a significant prayer experience you have had? What led up to it? Were you aware of God being present to you in some way? Can you talk about it to a close friend? Go back and relive it in as detailed a way as you can.

Notes

1. George A. Maloney SJ, *The Breath of the Mystic*, Dimension Books, Denville, New Jersey, 1974, p. 7.
2. Paul Murray OP, *The Mysticism Debate*, Franciscan Herald Press, Chicago, Illinois, 1977, p. 23.
3. Harvey D. Egan SJ, *Christian Mysticism*, Pueblo, New York, 1984, p. 248.

Reading List

George A. Maloney SJ, *The Breath of the Mystic*, Dimension Books, Denville, New Jersey, 1974.
Harvey D. Egan SJ, *Christian Mysticism*, Pueblo Publishing Company, New York, 1984.
Evelyn Underhill, *Practical Mysticism*, Ariel Press, Columbus, Ohio, 1986.
Aug. Poulain SJ, *The Graces of Interior Prayer*, Kegan Paul, Trench, Trübner & Co Ltd., London, 1910.
William Johnston, *The Wounded Stag*, Collins Fount Paperbacks, London, 1985.
Thomas Merton, *Seeds of Contemplation*, New Directions, New York, 1986.

PART II

Introduction

The following chapters introduce mystics who cover part of the wide range of Christian mysticism.

The remarkable twelfth-century German visionary, Hildegard of Bingen, is a model of the liberated woman concerned with issues that are highly relevant today, such as justice, women's rights and love and respect for our environment.

'The Cloud of Unknowing' and St John of the Cross illustrate the apophatic tradition of praying without words, concepts, images. Because of the growing interest in and influence of Eastern methods, I feel it is important to draw attention to the big part this so-called negative way plays in our Christian prayer.

To balance these are two very influential teachers of prayer, St Ignatius Loyola and St Teresa of Jesus. Both are normally classed as kataphatic, since they follow the affirmative way of using words, concepts and images in prayer. Most of us probably began our journey in prayer along these lines.

Julian of Norwich chose herself, since her simple teaching is so attractive and relevant to our modern world's search for God.

Three other spiritual writers whose works are popular today are St Francis de Sales, Jean-Pierre de Caussade and Thomas Merton. These seem to me to encourage the everyday, ordinary mystics that Karl Rahner and William Johnston write about.

Mother Mary MacKillop provides us with the example of how a person is formed for intimacy with Jesus in the paschal mystery. She belongs to the twentieth century, is an ordinary person, and very open about her prayer.

I have chosen to write about Gerry Pieper SJ because his prayer-journey enriched mine and I wanted to pay tribute to a contemporary martyr.

Finally, Mary the first Christian mystic. She sums up in her life the passionate encounter with a passionate God that is at the heart of mysticism.

13.

Hildegard of Bingen

A Feather on the Breath of God

> Listen, there was once a king sitting on his throne. Around him stood great and wonderfully beautiful columns ornamented with ivory, bearing the banners of the king with great honour. Then it pleased the king to raise a small feather from the ground and he commanded it to fly. The feather flew, not because of anything in itself but because the air bore it along. Thus am I . . .[1]

In that beautiful poetic image Hildegard describes herself. She was born in 1098, the youngest of ten children, at Bockelheim, in the diocese of Mainz, Germany. At the age of eight she was placed under the care of a woman called Jutta of Spanheim, who lived close by the Benedictine monastery at Disibode. In 1112 this Jutta became the leader of a community of women attached to this monastery. At about the age of eighteen, Hildegard took the Benedictine habit, and when Jutta died in 1136 she was elected abbess of the growing community of women.

When she was forty-two years and seven months old—as she tells us with that same attention to detail that Julian of Norwich much later used in describing her spiritual awakening—Hildegard was told in a vision, 'Write what you see and hear. Tell people how to enter the kingdom of salvation'.[2] Visions were not new to her, but this one is the first of which we have a record. It disturbed her and undermined her health, which was only restored when she began to obey.

In 1147 Hildegard and her sisters left Disibode and entered a new cloister in Rupertsberg near today's town of Bingen. That same year *Scivias* was completed. The first major book she wrote, it took ten years to finish and describes twenty-six visions. During the writing it was approved by the Trier Synod (30 November 1147—mid-February 1148), when Pope Eugene III read part of it to the gathering. Bernard of Clairvaux supported Hildegard and the pope encouraged her to continue.

Hildegard continued telling people 'how to enter the kingdom of salvation', whether they were popes, archbishops, abbots, kings, emperors, monks, sisters or laity. This she did by letters, for, like Catherine of Siena, she was a prolific letterwriter. Around 145 letters are extant, the first sent to St Bernard of Clairvaux in 1147. She was troubled about her visions and asked the saint to help her.

'Gentle father,' she wrote, 'you are so secure, answer me in your goodness, me, your unworthy servant girl, who from childhood has never, not even for one single hour, lived in security.'[3]

St Bernard must have reassured her, for near the end of 1153 she challenged, in no uncertain terms, the eighty-year-old Pope Anastasius IV:

> And why do you not cut out the roots of the evil which chokes the good, useful, fine-tasting, sweet-smelling plants? You are neglecting justice, (which is) the king's daughter, the heavenly bride, the woman who was entrusted to you. And you are even tolerant that this princess be hurled to the ground. Her crown and jewelled raiments are torn to pieces through the moral crudeness of men who bark like dogs and make stupid sounds like chickens which sometimes begin to cackle in the middle of the night. They are hypocrites.[4]

Besides her legacy of letters, we have the books she wrote. *Scivias*, the first of the three books that described her visions, took its title from the Latin exhortation, 'Know the ways'. The book has three parts: part I treats of God the Father and Creator; part II looks at the Saviour and Redemption; and part III is concerned with the Holy Spirit. In an introduction, Hildegard writes of a burning light poured into her mind so that she was able to understand the scriptures suddenly.

The dynamic is threefold: a description of what she sees and hears, a commentary on the meaning, and a painting done under her strict supervision.

The second book of the visionary trilogy was begun in 1158 and completed in 1163. It is called *The Book of Life's Merits* and is a moral treatise.

The Book of Divine Works, written between 1163 and 1173, rounds off the trilogy. This contains 'Ten Visions of God's Deeds in the World and Humanity'. In the foreword Hildegard says that she was in her fifty-sixth year when she 'had a vision so deep and overpowering that I trembled over my whole body and began to fall ill because of my bodily weakness'.[5] Again she was commanded to transmit what 'you see with your inner eye and what you hear with the inner ear of your soul'.

Besides these books, she wrote *Nine Books on the Subtleties of the Different Kinds of Creatures*—a scientific and medical encyclopedia to which is added a *Book of Compound Medicine*—and a collection of liturgical poetry and music, entitled *Symphony of Celestial Revelations.*

Some smaller lives of saints, seventy-two songs and a morality play set to music (the first of its kind) round off a most impressive literary output. Moreover, although Hildegard suffered several severe illnesses, she founded two monasteries and completed four arduous teaching journeys.

This first German woman mystic was actively involved in the major political and religious issues of the twelfth century: the Crusades; the struggle between empire and papacy; the Cathar heresy, which was teaching dualism with its two principles of good and evil in the world; and the rights of women religious.

No wonder, then, that Pope John Paul II called Hildegard 'a light to her people and her time [who] shines out more brightly today'.[6]

> Till a lioness arose breasting the babble,
> A prophetess towered in the tumult, a virginal tongue told.[7]

Thus Gerard Manley Hopkins pictures the heroic nun in 'The Wreck of the Deutschland', lines that capture the life and the achievements of Hildegard of Bingen. Her letters, the descriptions of her visions, her poetry, her music, her knowledge of science and medicine, her linking of science and religion and her labours for renewal made her a beacon for her times, a prophetess who towered in the tumult, a mystic who 'reared herself to divine ears' and who found her Christ in the 'black-about-air'.

Pope John Paul also said that she shines out more brightly today. Reflection on the legacy she has left the Church and the world shows how true that is.

Justice is an issue that dominates today, and it was very dear to the heart of Hildegard. Vision 10 of the *Book of Divine Works* describes the struggle between Divine Justice and Evil,[8] Hildegard's letter to Pope Anastasius bluntly accuses him of neglecting justice,[9] her letter to King Konrad III unflinchingly summons him to his obligations to 'lead your kingdom and carefully show your people every justice so that you will not depart from the divine kingdom'.[10] Barbarossa is told to rule with the sceptre of compassion, and to be an armed fighter who bravely withstands the devil, to cast off all greed and choose moderation, 'For that is what the highest King loves'.[11]

King Henry II was crowned King of England in 1154. Religious strife divided his kingdom, and this led eventually to the murder of Thomas à Becket in 1170. Henry repented, but before he did so Hildegard wrote him a beautifully encouraging letter summoning him to repentance. She speaks of a bird as black as pitch, flying out of midnight, tempting him to do what he wants and urging him not to be a slave of justice. 'Be resolute,' she continues, 'and fly those entanglements, beloved son of God, and call to God! God will gladly stretch out a hand to help you. Now live forever and remain in eternal blessedness.'[12]

It is not only the high and mighty who were Hildegard's concern. She reached out in love to her own sisters, to clergy and members of religious communities, and to the laity. In fact, one of her most consoling letters reminds the laity that they too are called to love and serve faithfully 'the guiltless Lamb of God who embraced you with great love'.[13]

'The trumpet of the Lord is the justice of God that you should deeply consider with great zeal in holiness,' she wrote to the clergy at Cologne.[14] She sounds the same clarion call to our own times.

Another theme that makes her so relevant to us is that of the rights of women. Pope Paul VI declared St Teresa of Jesus and St Catherine of Siena doctors of the Church. Pope John Paul II highly praised Hildegard. These recognitions are most welcome but there is still much to be done if the voices of women are to be more widely heard and their wisdom absorbed.

There is an awakening today to the lopsidedness that results when a man is not balanced by that female part that Jung has named the anima, and when the operation of the right-hand side of the brain is neglected. Hildegard experienced the power structure of a patriarchal Church, and she fought it. Moving the sisters of Rupertsberg was achieved in the face of strong opposition from the male community at Disibode.

Towards the end of her life, Hildegard and her community were placed under an interdict, which forbade them the Eucharist and Office in Choir, because they had allowed a young excommunicated nobleman to be buried in the church cemetery. The man had been reconciled before his death, and Hildegard saw that it would be an injustice to allow the prelates of Mainz to remove the body to the Rupertsberg cemetery. It was her final battle for justice, and she succeeded in having the interdict lifted. Her letters to the prelates of Mainz and Archbishop Christian tell of her struggle and her defence of the rights of the community and the dead man.[15]

The Church today must hear the voice of valiant women like Hildegard, and it is providential that this prophetess for today is being rediscovered.

The times she lived in were most troubled, and yet she rose above them by her exuberant celebration of life. Colour and light fill her writings and her paintings. She used bright green as a symbol of growth and life. Green virtues, green justice, green power keep reminding us of the rich world that God has given us.[16]

The third vision of *Scivias,* part I, shows the universe as an egg.[17] The mandala form, the warm subdued colours and the variety of symbols lead us into the mystery of creation. Twenty-eight years later, in the second vision of the *Book of Divine Works* Hildegard would depict the universe as a circle, a giant wheel in the centre of which is a human figure.[18] Now the colours are brighter, with lovely shadings of blue. The mandala is more pronounced. Animals, plants, stars, black fire, luminous fire and watery air are all to be seen in this captivating vision.

Here is a mystic who, like her God, is in love with the earth and who, like Teilhard de Chardin, sings hymns of praise to God for his creation. It comes as no surprise, then, that she strongly opposed the Cathar heresy, with its rejection of the material as evil.

The modern call to repentance for our sins against the earth and our neglect of the gift of God's rich creation finds a patron in this remarkable twelfth-century visionary.

Developments in prayer have led many to the use of the mandala, and this has taken them into Eastern prayer practices. Few know of the Western mystic Hildegard's use of the mandala. Her illustrations abound with the imagery of the wheel, the circle of the mandala, as in the second vision of the second part of *Scivias.*[19] Gazing contemplatively on this mandala, the wheel of God, the Trinity, may bring the experience that 'God hugs you. You are encircled by the arms of the mystery of God'.[20] You are enfolded by love, as Julian of Norwich said much later.

Both of these women mystics lead us into the mystery of the maternity of God. Prayer, for them, is an encounter, not a performance.

Finally, in modern times there is a rediscovery of healing and spiritual direction as ways towards wholeness. On this subject, too, Hildegard speaks.

She was asked what should be done with someone who wants to receive Communion but suffers from frequent bouts of vomiting. In response, Hildegard said the Sacrament should not be offered. The priest, however, should hold the host over the person's head and pray for healing, then hold the host over the heart of the sick person and pray again for the healing of body and soul, and for strengthening in faith.[21] Hildegard shows reverence for the Eucharist, strong faith and compassion.

In several of her letters there is the same balanced advice, as she talks about sin. She counsels Elizabeth, a young Benedictine nun, to moderation, which is the mother of all virtues, and urges her to be on guard against that 'pitch black bird, the devil', who through temptations to excessive penitential practices leads a person to a life without hope, without joy. How clearly she is alert to the deceits of the devil disguised as an angel of light! Ignatius, in the cave of Manresa, could have done with the spiritual wisdom of Hildegard!

Letter 35 is well worth studying for all who desire to learn the art of discernment. Writing to an abbot seeking advice, Hildegard tells him to welcome a certain monk with compassion, give a moderate penance and exercise discretion, the mother of all virtues.[22]

There are three letters in particular in which Hildegard reveals something of her own fears and struggles. One is to Elizabeth, the young Benedictine nun who was also a visionary and was meeting with opposition to her visions. Hildegard writes: 'I am but a poor creature and fragile vessel, yet what I speak to you comes not from me but from the clear light'. Beautifully she encourages Elizabeth to allow God to blow the trumpet, as he does through her, Hildegard, 'even though I suffer from a heart of little courage and am again and again disturbed and crippled by fear'.[23]

The other two letters are to a Benedictine monk, Wibert of Gembloux. Again Hildegard testifies to God speaking through her visions, and describes them. In true humility she praises God, who works where he will. As for herself:

> I am continuously filled with fear and trembling. For I do not recognize in myself security through any kind of personal ability. And yet I raise

> my hands aloft to God, just like a feather which has no weight from its own strength and lets itself be carried by the wind.[24]

In 1179 God's feather died at the age of eighty-one. Today she returns as an ideal model of the liberated woman to challenge us all.

Reflections

1. Settle down before the first 'Illumination' in the collection put together by Matthew Fox, *The Man in Sapphire Blue: A Study in Compassion.* (This is the second vision of the second part of *Scivias.*) Contemplate the mandala without trying to work out its meaning. Just allow Hildegard to speak to you through the colours and design of the painting.

2. Catherine of Siena says that when God saw how beautiful his creation was, he fell helplessly in love with it. Take a flower and keep looking and looking at it until you eventually see it. Have you any sense of being one with the flower? Do you think that Hildegard can help you in your prayer? In your attitudes to life, to the world? Is it the paintings or the descriptions of her visions that appeal to you?

3. Hildegard was very fond of symbols. Seek out some symbols she used. Consider the symbol that for you best expresses God, Jesus, the Holy Spirit, Mary. When you have chosen one, look carefully at it and listen to what it has to say to you. Continue the dialogue for as long as you and the symbol wish.

4. Elizabeth Dreyer writes of Hildegard as a passionate woman. God is sometimes described as a passionate God. Is your experience of God a passionate relationship?

5. Many today see Hildegard as a prophetess for our times. Reflect on her message. What current issues addressed by Hildegard interest you the most?

Notes

1. Quoted in the notes on the cassette recording, 'A Feather on the Breath of God'. Hyperion: KA 66039.
2. Hildegard of Bingen, *Scivias*, Bear & Company, Santa Fe, New Mexico, 1986, p. ix.
3. Hildegard of Bingen, *Book of Divine Works with Letters and Songs*, Bear & Company, Santa Fe, New Mexico, 1987, p. 271.
4. ibid., p. 274.
5. ibid., p. 5.
6. Quoted from L'Osservatore Romano, 1 October 1979, by Matthew Fox in *Illuminations*, Bear & Company, Santa Fe, New Mexico, 1985, p. 9.
7. Gerard Manley Hopkins, 'The Wreck of the Deutschland', *The Poems of Gerard Manley Hopkins*, edited by Robert Bridges, 2nd edition, Oxford University Press, London, 1933, p. 17.
8. *Book of Divine Works*, p. 222.
9. ibid., p. 273.
10. ibid., p. 288.
11. ibid., p. 289.
12. ibid., p. 293.
13. ibid., p. 342.
14. ibid., p. 322.
15. ibid., pp. 354–362.
16. ibid., p. 307.
17. *Scivias*, p. 27.
18. *Book of Divine Works*, p. 22.
19. *Scivias*, p. 87.
20. Gabriele Uhlein, *Meditations with Hildegard of Bingen*, Bear & Company, Santa Fe, New Mexico, 1983, p. 90.
21. *Book of Divine Works*, p. 335.
22. ibid., p. 334.
23. ibid., pp. 338, 340.
24. ibid., pp. 347–354.

Reading List

Gabriele Uhlein, *Meditations with Hildegard of Bingen*, Bear & Company, Santa Fe, New Mexico, 1983.

Illuminations of Hildegard of Bingen, Bear & Company, Santa Fe, New Mexico, 1985.

Elizabeth Dreyer, *Passionate Women*, Paulist Press, New York, 1989.

Hildegard of Bingen, *Scivias*, Bear & Company, Santa Fe, New Mexico, 1986.

Hildegard of Bingen, *Book of Divine Works with Letters and Songs*, Bear & Company, Santa Fe, New Mexico, 1987.

Sabina Flanagan, *Hildegard of Bingen, A Visionary Life*, Routledge, London, 1989.

14.

'The Cloud of Unknowing'

The Dark Way

The Cloud of Unknowing is a classic of Christian mysticism that is enjoying a great popularity today and exerting a strong influence on modern approaches to prayer. Its author is an unknown Englishman, a priest, a director of souls and probably a religious. But, like the *Imitation of Christ,* often ascribed to Thomas à Kempis, *The Cloud* was published anonymously.

It seems to have been written during the second half of the fourteenth century and is part of the remarkable writings on mysticism of that time that include Julian of Norwich, Walter Hilton, Richard Rolle, Catherine of Siena, Meister Eckhart and John Tauler. The *Imitation of Christ* comes from approximately the same time: Thomas à Kempis was born in 1370 or 1380 and died in 1471. So *The Cloud* was written during a time of rich flowering in mystical prayer.

The history of those times reveals political, social and military unrest (the Hundred Years War, the Black Death, the English peasants' revolt, the Captivity of Avignon, the Western Schism, Lollardy and Wycliffe in England.) Yet no reference is made in *The Cloud* to these upheavals. The thirteenth century witnessed the great Scholastic Age of Thomas

Aquinas and Bonaventure. In England the fourteenth century was the age of Chaucer—Merrie England.

Besides *The Cloud*, the anonymous author wrote *The Book of Privy Counselling*, which has been called a postscript to *The Cloud* and reflects the author's growth in maturity and certainty, and five other treatises: *Denis Hid Divinity, Benjamin,* the *Epistle of Prayer,* the *Epistle of Discretion,* and the *Epistle of Discerning of Spirits.*

The Cloud of Unknowing is addressed to a disciple aged twenty-four, but possibly this is a literary device, which makes no difference to our understanding of its teaching on contemplative prayer.

It belongs to the apophatic tradition, which stretches from Gregory of Nyssa to its climax with John of the Cross.

You will find little about psychic phenomena in *The Cloud,* except to warn against pseudo-mysticism. What the author is interested in is the intense encounter with God who loves us passionately and who unites us with himself in a loving, illuminating, purifying, transforming and gratuitous gift. This is the essence of true mysticism.

The book's full title is *A Book on Contemplation called The Cloud of Unknowing, which is about that cloud within which one is united to God.* The author provides a prayer addressed to God, a foreword and an introduction to the reader. He begins with a warning that the book is only for those deeply committed to following Christ in active and contemplative ways. These followers of Christ are to take time to read the book thoroughly, not out of idle curiosity.

The author then asks for God's help:

O God to whom all hearts lie open
to whom desire is eloquent
and from whom no secret thing is hidden,
purify the thoughts of my heart
by the outpouring of your spirit
that I may love you with a perfect love
and praise you as you deserve. Amen.

Very simply and directly the author says that the Lord has called you from the *common* way of Christian life to be his friend and to live the interior life in a *special* way. This desire he binds fast with the leash of love's longings. ('Fired with love's urgent longings,' wrote John of the Cross about two hundred years later.) Gently and kindly God has drawn you into the *singular* way of life, and you now live at the deep solitary core of your being.

This stage is marked by a strong desire for God, which is the sign of the call to contemplation. It is a pure gift from God. In humility this must be seen, and you must keep nourishing in your heart the lively longing for God. The focus is on the will, the faculty of desire, and the contemplative moment happens when the will is united with God.

In chapter 3 there is a clear description of this work of contemplation:

> This is what you are to do: lift your heart up to the Lord, with a gentle stirring of love, desiring him for his own sake and not for his gifts. Centre all your attention and desire on him and let this be the sole concern of your mind and heart. Do all in your power to forget everything else, keeping your thoughts and desires free from involvement with any of God's creatures or their affairs, whether in general or in particular. Perhaps this will seem like an irresponsible attitude, but I tell you, let them all be; pay no attention to them.

The stirring of love is gentle, as the heart awakens to God, surrendering to his love, desiring only God himself. Vigorous effort is to be avoided, but you are to persevere diligently until you feel the joy of it. Usually nothing is felt at first but a kind of darkness about your mind, 'as it were, a cloud of unknowing'. Learn to be at home in this darkness, aware only of a naked intent towards God in the depths of your being. John of the Cross discusses more fully and scientifically the nature of this cloud of unknowing when he writes of the active and passive nights of the senses and the spirit. The author of *The Cloud* just says it is darkness, the absence of knowledge, and is at pains to avoid misunderstanding of this darkness:

> Do not suppose that because I have spoken of darkness and of a cloud, I have in mind the clouds you see in an overcast sky or the darkness of your house when your candle fails. If I had, you could with a little imagination picture the summer skies breaking through the clouds or a clear light brightening the dark winter. But this isn't what I mean at all so forget this sort of nonsense. When I speak of darkness, I mean the absence of knowledge. If you are unable to understand something or if you have forgotten it, are you not in the dark as regards this thing? You cannot see it with your mind's eye. Well, in the same way, I have not said 'cloud,' but cloud of unknowing. For it is a darkness of unknowing that lies between you and your God.

So it is not the intellect, nor the imagination, that unites us with God.

It is this darkness, this cloud, that is between you and your God, and only the naked intent of the will, 'the spontaneous desire, springing suddenly towards God like spark from a fire', can penetrate the darkness and unite the soul with God through love. The desire, movement and intent of the will are called naked because they occur without thoughts from the intellect or images from the imagination. So the desire is spontaneous and the contemplative union can happen in a flash. Clearly the author is describing infused, not acquired contemplation.

The activities of the mind and the imagination must be pushed down into the cloud of forgetting. All thoughts, no matter how good or holy, all words, all images, must be abandoned, consigned to the cloud of forgetting. The author is not anti-intellectual: the intellect is transcended not despised, because we cannot know God through thinking or be united to him by thought. It is only by loving desire that we can be one with him.

> Thought cannot comprehend God. And so, I prefer to abandon all I can know, choosing rather to love him whom I cannot know. Though we cannot know him, we can love him. By love he may be touched and embraced, never by thought. Of course, we do well at times to ponder God's majesty or kindness for the insight these meditations may bring. But in the real contemplative work, you must set all this aside and cover it over with a cloud of forgetting. Then let your loving desire, gracious and devout, step bravely and joyfully beyond it and reach out to pierce the darkness above. Yes, beat upon that thick cloud of unknowing with the dart of your loving desire and do not cease, come what may.

It is ironic and typically paradoxical that the prayer which discards all images is described by the images of two clouds—the cloud of unknowing and the cloud of forgetting.

Chapter 7 is very helpful for understanding the nature of this contemplation:

> Whenever you feel drawn by grace to the contemplative work and are determined to do it, simply raise your heart to God with a gentle stirring of love . . . A naked intent towards God, the desire for him alone, is enough.

Choose a one syllable word like 'God' or 'love', one that is meaningful to you and sums up all your desire, and use this to steady and empty your mind and imagination. There is an amusing description of the power of one word in the cry for 'Help!' or 'Fire!'. Let this one-syllable word bubble up within you. When your mind is steady and empty, let go of your word.

Genuine contemplation is simply a spontaneous desire, springing suddenly towards God like spark from a fire. It comes from a sincere, humble heart. Daydreaming, fantasising or subtle reasoning are not this true contemplation. The faculties of the mind and the imagination are to be at peace, for this deep gift of contemplation is divinely infused, not acquired by human effort.

There are times, of course, when meditating on God's attributes, for example, or on the Passion of Jesus, are helpful, but not when God is inviting you into this contemplative union. When that happens, everything else must yield, because one loving, blind desire for God alone is more valuable than anything you can produce by meditation.

The author writes beautifully about perfect humility, and about how this contemplative loving of God by the simple naked thrusting of the will towards God hidden in the Cloud of Unknowing brings us to humility. Likewise his teaching on sin: by clinging in love and longing to the cloud of unknowing, Mary Magdalene avoided the trap of being mesmerised by the cesspool of her sins. Over-anxiety about our sins can absorb our attention. By taking two little words 'God' and 'sin' and alternating them, instead of examining your sins in detail, you will grow in virtue, and God alone will hold sway in your mind and heart. It should be remembered, however, that he is presuming a person's sins have been forgiven in the Sacrament of Reconciliation before he or she enters into the contemplative life that God is offering.

He speaks in paradoxes: 'Do not try to withdraw into yourself'. Be content to be nowhere, because nowhere, physically, is everywhere spiritually. Never mind that your mind chides you for doing nothing—go with this nothing, moved only by your love of God. This nothingness is blessed. John of the Cross wrote about no-thing: *nada, nada.* It is the superficial self that derides this as emptiness. Our true, inner self appreciates it as a fullness beyond measure. 'How wonderfully is a man's love transformed by the interior experience of this nothingness and this nowhere.'

The final chapter warns again that not all who read this book and find it interesting are therefore called to this infused contemplation. The inner excitement may be caused by curiosity. There are two signs that help us discern whether God is inviting us into the darkness. First a person must have done all in his or her power to purify the conscience of deliberate sin, according to the precepts of Holy Church and the advice of a spiritual director. Secondly, is he or she habitually more attracted to this simple contemplative prayer than to any other spiritual devotion? John of the Cross elaborates on this in *The Ascent of Mount Carmel.* Our author here concludes by praising holy desires.

The Book of Privy Counselling is a rewarding sequel. Its teaching is more compressed and its treatment confirms the message of *The Cloud of Unknowing.*

Thomas Merton wrote: 'Indeed there has never been a book on mysticism that showed such realistic common sense as *The Cloud*—and the other writings of the same author'. It is this down-to-earth, common-sense approach to the difficult topic of mysticism that makes *The Cloud* so valuable.

The literary style is simple, graceful and persuasive. At times there is effective use of paradox to stop the reader from taking what has been said literally. The author speaks of playing games with God by hiding. I am reminded of the hide-and-seek games between the lover and the beloved that are described in the Song of Songs. His imagery can be very effective, ironically enough in a book about imageless prayer:

> Rely more on joyful enthusiasm then on sheer brute force.
>
> Wait with gracious and modest courtesy for the Lord's initiative and do not impatiently snatch at grace like a greedy greyhound suffering from starvation.

There is vigorous ridicule when the author is attacking pseudo-mysticism and students of necromancy. While the content of *The Cloud* reminds me of John of the Cross, the style suggests Teresa of Jesus and *The Way of The Pilgrim*.

This common-sense and clear readable style makes *The Cloud* very helpful for all who wish to discover something of the riches of Christian mysticism. Although the central focus is the supremacy of mystical infused contemplation as entry into loving union with God, it offers help for allowing the Spirit to lead us into prayer of the heart. All of this is presented in a fully Christian way with a loyal allegiance to the Church and sacramental life. The quicksands of the passivity of quietism (the notion that God does everything) are avoided, as the importance of meditation, of the sacramental forgiveness of sins, of following the example of Christ, of humility and of charity are all emphasised. Although there is not a great deal about kataphatic mystical prayer (unlike the writings of Teresa and Ignatius), the intellect and the imagination command healthy respect.

The pitfalls of pseudo-mysticism—seeking the experience for its own sake, stopping at the meeting with the self, withdrawing from life—are exposed. As Harvey Egan comments in *Christian Mysticism*, *The Cloud* makes it clear that purifying, illuminating, transforming and unifying love is what mysticism is all about.

The constant reminder that all prayer is a gift and that we are to wait patiently upon God is salutary because our culture is emphasising 'do it yourself' and 'love is a feeling'. True, God gives the grace, but some human effort, some active passivity, is needed. *The Cloud* never advocates complete passivity. Although the author appreciates the importance of emotions for prayer, and so encourages prayer from the heart, he knows that love is more than a feeling. The encounter with God brings about the union of wills. Spiritual consolation and joy are gratefully accepted, but we do not seek them for their own sake. God alone is the goal.

The Cloud is a good counter to inward journeys that stop at the self and do not encounter God. Hence it is very relevant for today.

> In *The Book of Privy Counselling*, the safeguards are summarized. God assists man through secondary means: the light of scripture, reliable counsel, and the dictates of common sense, which include the demands of one's state, age, and circumstances in life. In fact, in all ordinary activities a man must never pursue an inspiration—be it ever so pious or attractive—until he has rationally examined it in the light of these three witnesses.

Mysticism is in the air today, and many are seeking guides and gurus. Both *The Cloud* and *The Book of Privy Counselling* can be recommended as reliable reading. Although directed towards the dark, unknowing way of loving God, they contain solid instructions to help all in their prayer journeys.

Reflections

1. '. . . lovingly offering your blind, naked being to the glorious being of your God . . . Though they are distinct by nature, grace has made them one.' (*The Book of Privy Counselling*).

   How does the author avoid the danger of quietism?
   What is meant by 'blind', 'naked'?
   The mystic union is sometimes said to be pantheism. How does the author guard against that heresy?

2. If meditations make me weep for sorrow at Christ's Passion, why push them into the cloud of forgetting? Why abandon what is good? Reflect upon these objections to the contemplative prayer that is being described. (See chapter 8 of *The Cloud*.)

3. The author proposes Mary Magdalene as our model. What is there about Mary that best qualifies her for this role? Are you able to apply these characteristics to your own prayer life? Are you more comfortable with the role of Mary or Martha?

4. 'Anyone who aspires to contemplation ought to cultivate study, reflection, and prayer, or to put it differently, reading, thinking, and praying' (chapter 35). Why does the author recommend developing these three habits? Which do you think most requires your attention?

5. Reflect upon the snares used by the devil to hinder growth in contemplation (chapters 51–57). Compare this teaching with that given by St Ignatius Loyola in his Rules for the Discernment of Spirits. Good people are tempted by an evil masquerading as a good. Have you ever found that what started off as good turned sour? How did that come about?

6. 'It is not what you are nor what you have been that God sees with his all-merciful eyes, but what you desire to be. St Gregory declares that "all holy desires heighten in intensity with the delay of fulfilment, and desire which fades with delay was never holy desire at all." ' How does this teaching about 'desires' make you feel? Do you agree with St Gregory's statement? Can you apply it to some situation in your own life when the desire continued to grow? What about a desire you had which faded over time?

Notes

All references are to William Johnston's edition of *The Cloud of Unknowing* and *The Book of Privy Counselling*, Image Books, Doubleday, New York, 1973.

Reading List

William Johnston, *The Mysticism of the Cloud of Unknowing*, Religious Experience series No. 8, Anthony Clarke, Hertsfordshire, 1978.

Harvey D. Egan SJ, *Christian Mysticism*, Pueblo Publishing Company, Inc., New York, 1984.

15.

Julian of Norwich

'Love Is His Meaning'

Julian of Norwich was born in 1342 and died sometime after 1416. She is a contemporary of the unknown author of *The Cloud of Unknowing*. Both authors deal with mysticism, but they do so very differently. *The Cloud* is really a treatise, which teaches through description: in it, there is no explicit sharing of the author's own prayer experiences. Julian of Norwich, on the other hand, describes the revelations (often called the 'showings') she received and her ongoing reflections on them. It is not known whether she was a religious, or living at home with her mother at the time of her mystical experiences. We do not know when she became an anchoress, but she was a 'recluse atte Norwyche' by 1400, being supported in a cell by the church of St Julian and St Edward at Conisford (itself attached to the Benedictine community at Carrow). She was highly respected as a spiritual director.

The book describing her 'showings' was written in Middle English and is the first example of a spiritual book in English by a woman. Her style is very different from that of *The Cloud*, much warmer and more explicitly personal. *The Cloud* is written by a good teacher, able to communicate personally and attractively. Julian is also a teacher, but her theological doctrine is shown to come out of her mystical experiences. She is learned, clear, spontaneous and unaffected. Her descriptions are vivid and her eye for detail shows the gifts of a poet and an artist.

We do not find in her book the humour and paradoxes of *The Cloud*, nor the gossipy, rambling descriptions that are part of the charm of St Teresa of Jesus. Nor do we find the detached objectivity that characterises the account of revelations described by St Ignatius Loyola in *The Autobiography*. But there is such warmth and simplicity in Julian that I find myself agreeing wholeheartedly with Thomas Merton's mature reflections that once he discovered Julian of Norwich she took over from Teresa and John of the Cross.

Her theology shows that she was an obedient daughter of the Church with deep love of the Trinity. Her work is more explicitly Christocentric than *The Cloud*. The centrality of the suffering Jesus in her prayer foreshadows Ignatius and Teresa. Her devotion to God as Mother, and Jesus as Mother, heralds the modern movement to free women from an oppressive Church and society. Her mysticism is so modern that we might well say that, just as Thomas Merton was the spiritual leader of the 1960s, so Julian of Norwich is our guide for the final decades of the twentieth century. Finally, in an age which writes and talks a lot about love, her message that love is God's meaning is a beautiful beacon.

The revelations began on 13 May 1373. Some time earlier, Julian had asked for three gifts: 'The first was a recollection of the Passion. The second was bodily sickness. The third was to have, of God's gift, three wounds.' The first and second desires passed from her mind, but the third remained continually.

When she was 'thirty and a half years old' (how attentive she is to detail!) she became sick and seemed to be dying. She received the last rites and held the crucifix. Then in rapid succession she received sixteen 'showings', fifteen in the five hours from four to nine o'clock in the morning following the priest's visit. The sixteenth occurred the following night. She recovered her health and some time later wrote down what happened. This account is known as the Short Text.

Many years of prayer and reflection followed, and then Julian described her experiences again. This second account is called the Long Text. The conclusion to it was written in 1393, twenty years after the mystical experiences the book describes. Comparisons between the Short Text and the Long Text show how Julian's theology of mysticism was enriched by the years of prayer. In what follows I refer to the Long Text.

Chapter 1 gives us a summary of the sixteen revelations.

> This is a revelation of love which Jesus Christ, our endless bliss, made in sixteen showings, of which the first is about his precious crowning of thorns; and in this was contained and specified the blessed Trinity, with the incarnation and the union between God and man's soul, with many fair revelations and teachings of endless wisdom and love, in which all the revelations that follow are founded and connected.

St Teresa's Lenten experience of 1554, when she was praying before the crucifix, began her second conversion and mystical journey. In like manner, Julian begins the journey of her three desires, described above. The account is clear, precise, level-headed—there is no sign of hysteria or neuroticism. Julian has a clear awareness of the difference between the first two desires—they are conditional, and don't persist—and her third desire for the threefold wounds of contrition, compassion and longing. It is a good example of the discerning of spirits and reminds us of Ignatius Loyola's reflections on his early desires during his sickness. She notes, also, that 'this was not the ordinary practice of prayer'.

The account of her sickness (chapter 3) shows her conformity to God's will and obedience to the priest telling her to look on the crucifix.

> He set the cross before my face and said: 'I have brought the image of your saviour; look at it and take comfort from it.' It seemed to me that I was well, for my eyes were set upwards towards heaven, where I trusted that I by God's mercy was going; but nevertheless I agreed to fixing my eyes on the face of the crucifix if I could, and so I did, for it seemed to me that I would hold out longer with my eyes set in front of me rather than upwards.

She suffers intensely and thinks she is at the point of death. Suddenly all pain is taken from her 'by God's secret doing' and 'it came into my mind that I ought to wish for the second wound as a gift and grace from our Lord . . . I desired to suffer with him, living in my mortal body, as God would give me grace.' She is asking for compassion, not only bodily vision. This account reminds me of the intense sufferings and suffocating endured by St Therèse of the Child Jesus, so movingly recorded in her 'Last Conversations', and how she kissed the Face on the Cross, rather than the feet.

As Julian looked at 'the red blood running down from under the crown, hot and flowing freely and copiously', the Trinity filled her heart with the greatest joy. And she saw Our Lady, Mary, 'a simple, humble maiden, young in years'.

Julian speaks of three different kinds of visions she received. One is bodily sight, another is 'ghostly sight in bodily likeness', and a third is 'ghostly' sight. Paul Molinari SJ comments helpfully and refers to St Augustine's classical division into those that are corporeal (that is, known through the bodily external senses), those that are imaginary (that is, seen and recognised as such in the mind of the perceiver through the internal senses), and those that are intellectual (that is, fed into the soul by the direct action of God without the use of the senses). Molinari concludes that no particular kind predominates with Julian. As she reflects on her first revelation, she writes: 'All this was shown in three parts (different modes), that is to say, by bodily vision and by words formed in my understanding and by spiritual vision.' Three themes in Julian's visions seem to me to be relevant to our own day and may explain her popular appeal: they are her teachings about prayer, about sin, and about God as Mother.

Prayer

There is no better place for beginning this reflection than the opening of the fifth chapter.

> At the same time as I saw this sight of the head bleeding, our good Lord showed a spiritual sight of his familiar love. I saw that he is everything to us which is good and comforting for our help. He is our clothing, who wraps and enfolds us for love, embraces us and shelters us, surrounds us for his love, which is so tender that he may never desert us.

This God is creator, protector and lover, and only when we are united to him is true happiness found.

God's love is familiar, that is, homely and intimate. He is greatly pleased by the loving yearning of the soul through the touch of the Holy Spirit. God longs for this union and so does the soul. All this is a gift, and the union of wills, of desires, comes from his goodness.

Julian's God is surely the God who loves unconditionally. This fifth chapter enriches for me both the Foundation Exercise and the 'Take, O Lord, and Receive' prayer of the 'Contemplation for Attaining Divine Love', both in the *Spiritual Exercises* of Ignatius Loyola.

It seems that the vision of Our Lady, who pondered things in her heart and was the first Christian mystic, leads Julian into the beautiful contemplative prayer of this chapter five.

Desiring and seeking are at the heart of prayer. Julian distinguishes between seeking and finding. She learns that seeking is as good as finding (contemplating):

> Seeking is common to all, and every soul can have through grace and ought to have discretion and teaching from the Church.
>
> It is God's will that we receive three things from him as gifts, as we seek. The first is that we seek willingly and diligently . . . joyfully and happily . . . the second is that we wait for him steadfastly . . . the third is that we have great trust in him . . . And he wants to be trusted, for he is very accessible, familiar, and courteous. Blessed may he be.

Prayer, then, is a joyful search, a patient waiting and a trusting faith. Simone Weil, another intimate friend of God, described it as waiting patiently but with expectation for the coming of the Lord.

Julian's fourteenth revelation deals specifically with two conditions about prayer: it is to be rightful (that is, according to God's will) and show confident trust. Our trust is often not complete; we think that God may not hear us because of our unworthiness and because we are feeling nothing at all. Yet we should not be discouraged and should pray wholeheartedly:

> Though you may feel nothing, though you may see nothing, though you think that you could not pray. For in dryness and in barrenness, in sickness and in weakness—then is your prayer most pleasing to me, though you think it almost tasteless to you.

How clearly in this chapter and the next does Julian teach that prayer is not a performance, nor a feeling! It is God who is the ground of our praying. For Julian prayer is a living and growing relationship with the triune God in Jesus Christ. It unites the soul to God through the gift of our courteous Lord. When he takes over all our powers, all that we can do is contemplate him and rejoice. Chapter 43 seems to speak of contemplation strictly so called, in describing 'exalted and imperceptible prayer'.

Although Julian does not write a formal treatise on prayer, her revelations are packed with a rich and safe theology of prayer. Encountering a 'homely, loving God whose meaning is love', she finds strong hope, trust in God alone, deep joy. Her joy belongs to the harvest of the Spirit (Galatians 5: 22).

Her sickness is the occasion of her second conversion, calling her to contrition, compassion, and longing for God. She is led into a deep union of wills, understanding always, with John of the Cross, that this is a union that never destroys her identity. Her God, who is Father and

Mother, and who wraps her around with love, calls her into a loving union.

Sin

The description of the thirteenth revelation covers chapters 27 to 40. Julian gives us the fruits of enlightenment received over the years of contemplation, and in particular what was revealed to her about the mystery of sin. Many came to know of Julian through T.S. Eliot, who quoted her comment, 'Sin is necessary, but all will be well, and all will be well, every kind of thing will be well.'

As she recalls her longing for our Lord, she sees that sin is the only hindrance. In the past, 'in my folly', she had puzzled about sin and why God did not prevent it. We see the same tension now. She is told that sin is necessary, and contemplating the Passion brings consolation. Sin still remains a mystery that will not be understood until God unfolds for us in heaven the reason he allowed sin. The compassion of Christ for us filled her in part with compassion for all her fellow Christians. But she still wonders how all things can be well, because of the great harm done by sin. The Lord reveals that the glorious atonement made by Jesus for Adam's sin far outweighs the evil.

Gradually we note that she is being drawn from her concern about sin to God's love: 'And in this I was taught that we should rejoice only in our blessed saviour Jesus, and trust in him for everything'. The Spirit and the Church are her guides.

Nevertheless, she continues her reflections on 'all will be well,' and we see how spiritual desolation continues to oppress her. In the third revelation, she tells us that she saw that God does all well and there is no vision of sin. But in the thirteenth, she saw sin, and God said that all will be well. Her revelations throw her back on her faith and do not provide answers to the deep mystery of sin in God's world of love. The recurring message is that 'all will be well'. Her struggles to reduce the mystery to a problem that will then admit of answers are gently handled by God.

God showed Julian that sin will be no shame, but honour to men because of God's mercy. Her spiritual desolation began to yield as her 'understanding was lifted up to heaven'. God filled her with joy and she was made glad and happy in love.

How tenderly she writes of repentance! 'By contrition we are made clean, by compassion we are made ready, and by true longing for God we are made worthy. Peace and love are always in us, living and working, but we are not always in peace and love.' The supreme friendship of our courteous Lord tenderly protects us while we are in our sins.

It is through our falls that we discover 'the great and marvellous knowledge of love in God without end; for enduring and marvellous is that love which cannot and will not be broken because of offences'.

The message that sinfulness cannot destroy God's love is good news for modern man, who is sometimes reluctant to face sin and even reduces it to psychological aberrations. Julian's own struggles with the mystery of sin invite us to deep contrition, compassion, and longing for our God.

God as Mother

Julian was led more deeply into the compassionate, sensitive, tender love of God: 'And so I saw that God rejoices that he is our Father, and God rejoices that he is our true spouse and that our soul is his beloved wife'. As she focuses on the Trinitarian God's love for us, she exclaims that the deep wisdom of the Trinity is our Mother, in whom we are enclosed. She keeps returning to the motherhood of God and teaches three ways of contemplating motherhood in God: 'The first is the Foundation of our nature's creation; the second is his taking of our nature, where the motherhood of grace begins; the third is the motherhood at work.' This beautifully anticipates St Ignatius Loyola's 'Contemplation for Attaining Divine Love'. She writes of the motherhood of love (Creation) and the motherhood of mercy and grace (Incarnation and Redemption).

Julian did not invent the theme of God's motherhood. It is found in Isaiah and also in some of the Fathers, like Augustine and Anselm, and some of her contemporaries. 'What makes her contribution original, however, is the theological precision with which she applies this symbolism to the Trinitarian relationships,' writes Jean Leclercq OSB. Her theology is enriched by the delightful poetic imagery with which it is presented. Theology is often best served by poetry.

She also speaks of Jesus as our Mother because he feeds us with his own body and blood, as a mother feeds a newborn child from her body. So the mothering which Jesus received from Mary is derived from his own. Chapter 60 well merits long and prayerful reflection to absorb the true devotion it presents.

Julian of Norwich is deservedly popular in our times because she addresses the themes that engage us. Clearly, for her, love is not a feeling but a union of wills. A true, correct sense of sin as the denial of love, as a breaking of the covenant and not just a legal breech, needs to be rediscovered. Julian's theology of sin helps here. The search for the feminine and the movement to liberate women, who are oppressed in a male-dominated Church and society, find a powerful, sensitive voice in Julian of Norwich. Above all, she is a very safe guide in the mystical journey that calls to many of our contemporaries.

Reflections

1. God is creator, protector and lover. Read chapter 5 of *Showings* and reflect on this description of God. Do you think it is Trinitarian? In what ways does Julian's teaching in this chapter help you in your prayer?

2. Compare the teaching and style of Julian and *The Cloud*. Which helps you most in your operational image of God and your prayer? What is it that brings this about?

3. 'Seeking with faith, hope and love pleases Our Lord and finding pleases the soul and fills it full of joy.' 'Seeking is as good as contemplating.' Reflect upon these two quotations. What is your spontaneous reaction to each? In your experience have you found that your seeking is as good as contemplating?

4. Reflect upon Julian's teaching on the motherhood of God and the motherhood of Jesus. When I have discussed this with groups I have found that most people are happy with her teaching on the Motherhood of God, but uneasy about the Motherhood of Jesus. What is your reaction? Are you able to address Jesus as your Mother?

5. Sin teaches us who we are and who God is, says Julian. Can you recall an experience of facing your sinfulness and being encouraged? What did you learn about yourself and about God? Some people are afraid that if they look at their sinfulness they will be led into self-rejection and meet a condemning God. How does Julian handle this situation? How do you?

Notes

ll references are to Julian of Norwich, *Showings*, Classics of Western Spiritualilty series, Paulist Press, New York, 1978.

Reading List

aul Molinari SJ, *Julian of Norwich*, Longman, Green & Co., London, 1958.
ustin Cooper OMI, *Julian of Norwich: Reflections on Selected Texts*, St Paul Publications, Homebush, NSW, 1986.

16.

St Ignatius Loyola

The Making of a Mystic

Ignatius Loyola was a man of surprising contrasts. He had a penetrating intellect, immense strength of will, untiring energy, an aversion to anything that could be called fanatic or bizarre, dogged perseverance, and openness to change, coupled with an affectionate and pure love of God and neighbour. Like John of the Cross, he was filled with love's urgent longings.

He was a law-giver, administrator, leader, pastor and prayer guide. In all these areas his contribution to the Church has been very great. His Constitutions, his many letters, the small part of his Spiritual Diary that has survived, and his *Spiritual Exercises* give ample proof of this contribution, but above all testify to 'the force that through the green fuse drives the flower'.

Ignatius was a deep mystic, yet able to descend to minute, elementary details when instructing others in the life of prayer. This ability is evident in his letters and in the *Spiritual Exercises,* an extraordinary programme for beginners and those already proficient in prayer. Because of the insistence on the personal encounter between God and the retreatant his works have been criticised for putting too much emphasis on human effort, and, at the other extreme, of being infected with quietism and the teachings of the Alumbrados, those sixteenth-century Spanish pseudomystics who claimed to act always under the direct illumination of the Holy Spirit. These criticisms surely can be made only by those who have never given themselves to the *Exercises* in their entirety. Ignatius always avoided these two extremes.

The Cloud, John of the Cross and Julian of Norwich did not cater for beginners in prayer in the detailed way that Ignatius does. And yet, as Francis de Sales says, these *Spiritual Exercises* have formed more saints than they have letters: to mention a few, Francis Xavier, Peter Canisius, Robert Bellarmine, Aloysius Gonzaga, and Stanislaus Kostka were all formed by the *Exercises*. Closer to our own times, Mother Mary MacKillop can be added to the list.

Pius XI declared Ignatius Loyola the patron of retreats. Ignatius himself attached so much value to them that he said that the best gift he could give anybody was the gift of the *Spiritual Exercises*.

Ignatius' journey through life is well documented. We have his own autobiography, thousands of letters, the *Spiritual Exercises*, the fragment of his spiritual diary, and the Jesuit Constitutions. From all these we can follow the reforming, transforming, conforming experiences that mirror the dynamic of the *Exercises* and are being lived out by the pilgram, as he called himself. Thus we are privileged to see how God led Ignatius into mysticism.

He was born at Loyola in 1491, the youngest of thirteen children. As a young knight he sought honour and glory in battle. When he was thirty, he was wounded at Pamplona and taken to his home at Loyola, where he received the Last Sacraments, as his life was despaired of. This was on the feast of St John the Baptist. Four days later he unexpectedly began to recover. He tells us about it in his autobiography: 'Now, the sick man [Ignatius] was devoted to St Peter, and our Lord thus desired that his recovery begin that very midnight. His improvement progressed so well that after a few days he was pronounced to be out of danger.[1]

During his convalescence his conversion began. His leg set badly. 'Because he was determined to make a way for himself in the world, he could not tolerate such ugliness and thought it marred his appearance.'[2] So he ordered the excess flesh and bone to be cut away. His health was restored, but as he could not yet stand on the leg, he was forced to remain in bed. To pass the time away, he asked for books to read. The chivalrous romances of his choice were not available, so he was forced to read *The Life of Christ* and lives of saints. We can only marvel at how God was invading his life and using adversities for good. Ignatius, whose ambition had been for wordly honour, discovered a new goal, the heroics of Francis and Dominic. He would equal, even outdo, them in what they had done. This deep spirit of competition would be curbed as he developed his spirituality. Noting and reflecting on the feelings aroused in him by his reading formed his first lessons in discernment.

Our Lady and the Child Jesus appeared to him:

> One night as he lay sleepless, he clearly saw the likeness of Our Lady with the holy child Jesus, and because of this vision he enjoyed an excess of consolation for a remarkably long time. He felt so great a loathing for all his past life, especially for the deeds of the flesh, that it seemed to him all the images which had been previously imprinted on his mind were now erased.[3]

Pamplona to Loyola was the first stage of the pilgrim's journey into mysticism. We see here the seeds of the mysticism to which God was drawing him. The purgative, or cleansing, way of transformation had begun: so also had discernment, which became a distinctive part of his mature spirituality.

He was beginning to be moved by the *magis*, as it is called, the ever increasing desire to give himself more generously to his Lord, and God was becoming the supreme goal of his life. The Marian vision heralded his enduring love of Mary and later visions of guidance.

The soldier, the man of action and the born leader of men, now reduced to inactivity and dependence, left Loyola still bent on service, feeling impelled to do penance for his sins, still concerned with honour, but with a new orientation, a God-direction. He was a loner, seeking no companions, and he went to Montserrat, a famous Marian shrine, to lay his sword at the feet of the famed statue of the Black Virgin. Her knight was beginning to surrender.

At Manresa, in the south of Spain, in solitude, amid poverty and physical austerities, tried by temptations and scruples, Ignatius came closer to union with God. For almost a year, this was his school. The first four months were marked by many vocal prayers and penances. He even practised voluntary neglect of his fingernails and toenails—surely most difficult for the Spanish *hidalgo* who was so conscious of his appearance! Through all this, he enjoyed much spiritual consolation.

Then followed a time of temptations, scruples and spiritual desolation. Later he would incorporate what God taught him about these swings between consolation and desolation into the 'Rules for the Discernment of Spirits'. This is his ascent of Mount Carmel, the ongoing purification of the purgative way, so essential for any mystical call.

The third phase of Ignatius' wrestling with God was marked by great mystical graces as God invaded his soul. Intellectual visions of the Trinity, the creation of the world, the Eucharist, the humanity of Christ gave him a profound insight into his faith. He tells us that he received such a lucidity in understanding that during the course of his entire life nothing could ever equal what he learnt on the banks of the Cardoner, near Manresa. He realised, for example, that the serpentine vision that appeared to him, filling him with great joy but leaving him disconsolate, was not true spiritual consolation.

The gift of discerning love continued to purify his ambition and form his spiritual wisdom. The 'knight penitent' was being transformed into the 'knight apostolic' and when Ignatius left Manresa after his ten months he was becoming a man of the Church. He started giving the *Exercises* and was drawn to the care of the sick and the destitute, and to spiritual conversations—the kind of service that characterised the Society of Jesus later. His mysticism of service was emerging.

A pilgrimage to the Holy Land brought Ignatius confirmation and enlightenment. He learned that it was God's will that he should not remain in Jerusalem. What is striking about this is his flexibility and obedience to the voice of the Church. Already his mysticism was church related and he was discovering that obedience was the light for his way. The Christ-centredness of his spirituality, as seen in the fruit of Manresa and his *Spiritual Exercises,* was confirmed by his visit to Jerusalem.

The pilgrim returned to Barcelona still searching for God's will. At the age of thirty-four he returned to the classroom to study Latin, and gathered his first group together—four companions. Now he no longer walked alone in his poverty and service of the sick and poor. He moved to Alcala and Salamanca, spent forty-two days in prison, suspected of heresy, and was prohibited from speaking on matters of faith until he had studied theology for four years. Thus God continued to lead the pilgrim by adversity. He was teaching Ignatius to find him in all things, especially in trials, and inviting him into the paschal mystery.

His first group dissolved and he went to Paris, still the pilgrim searching for God's will. Each stage of his journey brought its own contribution to the mystic God was making. Later the Society would embrace poverty, gratuity of ministries, friendship, intense apostolic activity, group meetings and above all an indestructible love of Christ—all features of his first community.

At Barcelona he studied grammar, at Alcala the humanities, at Paris theology. In 1528 he was thirty-seven and had been on pilgrimage for seven years. Now study took priority over mystical experiences. After completing his BA at forty-one and his MA two years later, he returned to Spain to recover his health. By this time he had formed his third group (the second like the first, had been shortlived) who would constitute the Society of Jesus. They were brought together by the power of the *Spiritual Exercises.*

In 1537 the vision at La Storta occurred, on the road to Rome. Ignatius' description of it is brief:

> After he had been ordained priest, he decided to wait another year before celebrating Mass, preparing himself and praying to Our Lady to place him with her Son. One day, while praying in a church a few miles outside Rome, he felt a great change in his soul and so clearly did he see God the Father place him with Christ, His Son, that he had no doubts that God the Father *did* place him with His Son.[4]

The Father placed Ignatius with Jesus carrying his Cross, and he understood that his Society had been accepted into the service of the Lord.

The vision at La Storta seemed to set the seal of the Father's approval on Ignatius' mysticism, which was definitely Trinitarian, Christ-centred, church-centred and Marian. His calling was to be a contemplative in action, serving the Church in apostolic activity, under the shadow of the Cross. It is a mysticism of service that draws him into the loving union of the paschal mystery.

Rome was journey's end for the pilgrim. The Society was approved in 1540 and Ignatius was elected its first General in 1541. Until his death in 1556 at the age of sixty-five his mysticism was one of service, as he administered the rapidly expanding, far-flung Society of Jesus. He had been forty-four years in preparation and twenty-one years in his final apostolate.

The mysticism of Ignatius Loyola belongs to the kataphatic tradition, unlike that of *The Cloud* and John of the Cross, but rather like that of Teresa of Jesus. The *Spiritual Exercises* present ways of praying through words and images. Through repetition, reflective discerning, and application of the senses, there is a lessening of conceptual prayer. The contemplative moment when the soul is lost in God and united directly with him happens as the images yield to the grace of the Spirit. The images are transparent, as is the light by which one sees objects.

There is no conscious forgetting or unknowing, as is advised in *The Cloud of Unknowing*.

The application of senses is the peak of the daily prayer dynamic in the *Spiritual Exercises*. The term may be misleading if it suggests effort, whereas the deep experience is a consequence of being saturated intellectually, emotionally and spiritually with the meditation or contemplation. 'Senses' means first of all the physical senses. Then we have imaginative senses: I can smell, taste, hear, see and touch in the imagination. At times I may be speaking of metaphorical senses, as Ignatius seems to be when he speaks of smelling the infinite fragrance of the Divinity. Ultimately there are the spiritual senses of mysticism that Origen and Augustine speak of, the senses of the heart.

Ignatius was very much a man of the senses. After the purgative way of the first week of the *Exercises,* he reminds the retreatant daily of this prayer of the senses which, with God's grace, may prove an entry into deep contemplation in the strict sense. The concluding prayer, the contemplation for attaining divine love, appeals to the senses, and to the heart; it reveals to us that distinguishing feature of the mysticism of Ignatius.

The mysticism of *The Song of Songs,* John of the Cross and Teresa of Jesus, is a bridal mysticism, as it speaks of spiritual betrothal and mystical marriage. The whole of Ignatius' journey was a searching for the will of God, so that his life might be spent in his service. He was a contemplative in action, seeking to find and serve God in all things. Service rather than union was what drove him on.

The few pages we have of his spiritual diary (from 13 March 1544 to 27 February 1545) have been called a discernment log book, since they record the experiences he had as he prayed about the poverty of the Society. It is a more personally revealing document than his autobiography, and it gives us a deeper awareness of the mystic God has formed. Clearly the Trinity is central to Ignatius' mysticism.

Ignatius Loyola is a mystic in the truest sense. He is also a mystic of everyday life, as his union with God pervades his daily work. When we consider his arduous journey and the adversities that purified his intentions, we may also see him as one invited into the paschal mystery.

Reflections

1. 'The Spiritual Diary is perhaps the most remarkable mystical document on Trinitarian mysticism ever written in any language.'—Harvey D. Egan SJ.

   Compare the Trinitarian mysticism of Ignatius as shown in the 'Contemplation for Attaining Divine Love' at the end of the *Spiritual Exercises* with that of Julian of Norwich. Which do you find more attractive? Do you find that either helps you in your prayer?

2. Harvey Egan describes the mystical graces of Ignatius as a sacramental mysticism of service, reverential love, and the Cross. Reflect on his statement. What evidence for it do you find in the life of Ignatius? Some see all of this as being far above them. What is your experience?

3. Ignatius gave the Church two sets of rules for the discernment of spirits. In his own life he was continually discerning the will of God. Distinguish between the discerning of spirits and discerning the will of God.

   Once somebody said to me that this was all too complicated: we should just trust God. Do you agree, or do you think there is a place today for Ignatius' teaching on discernment?

4. Ignatius wrote, 'In time of spiritual desolation we should never make any change'. Can you recall a time in your own life when you were thinking of making a change while in spiritual desolation? Reflect on your experience. Do you think this rule is a helpful one?

5. The following prayer for generosity is often associated with Ignatius:

   > Dearest Lord, teach me to be generous,
   > to give and not to count the cost,
   > to fight and not to heed the wounds,
   > to toil and not to seek for rest,
   > to labour and not to ask reward,
   > except that of knowing that I do your holy will.

   Say it slowly and prayerfully.

   Some are helped by body movement, by dancing a prayer and conveying their thoughts and feelings by gestures. Do you find an encounter with God by dancing this prayer, or any other?

Notes

1. *A Pilgrim's Journey: The Autobiography of Ignatius Loyola*, translation, with notes, by Joseph N. Tylenda SJ, Michael Glazier, Wilmington, Delaware, 1985, p. 10.
2. ibid., pp. 10, 11.
3. ibid., p. 16.
4. ibid., p.. 113.

Reading List

A Pilgrim's Journey: The Autobiography of Ignatius Loyola, translation, with notes, by Joseph N. Tylenda SJ, Michael Glazier, Wilmington, Delaware, 1985.

Hugo Rahner, *The Spirituality of St Ignatius Loyola*, Loyola University Press, Chicago, Illinois, 1980.

Harvey D. Egan SJ, *Ignatius Loyola The Mystic*, Michael Glazier, Wilmington, Delaware, 1987.

Joseph de Guibert SJ, *The Jesuits: Their Spiritual Doctrine and Practice*, Loyola University Press, Chicago, Illinois, 1964.

Fredrich Wulf (ed.), *Ignatius Loyola, His Personality and Spiritual Heritage*, The Institute of Jesuit Sources, St Louis, Missouri, 1977.

17.

St John of the Cross

The Living Flame of Love

St John of the Cross was born in 1542 at Fortiveros, in Spain. For four years he attended the Jesuit College in Medina del Campo, where he received a solid grounding in Latin and Greek. During these school days he also worked at the hospital. At the age of twenty-one he entered the Carmelite order and he was ordained a priest in 1567. He was drawn to join the Carthusians, but Mother Teresa of Avila interested him in a reform movement to restore the Primitive Rule of the Carmelites.

When they met he was twenty-five and Teresa fifty-two. As confessor to the Convent of the Incarnation, he guided her in her prayer. She had been led into mystic prayer after her Lenten second conversion experience eighteen years before, but not until John of the Cross became her guide did she receive the favour of Spiritual Marriage, as is called the ultimate union described in *The Interior Castle*.

In 1577 John was seized and taken away from Incarnation by Carmelites who opposed the Reform. Taken to Toledo, he was imprisoned for six months and scourged, to try to make him renounce the Reform. While in prison he composed thirty-one stanzas of *The Spiritual Canticle*. He escaped from prison and until 1591 continued to work for the Reform.

The last year of his life was marked by much opposition and suffering. He was forty-nine when he died, saying, 'Into your hands, O Lord, I commend my spirit'. Teresa had died in 1582, nine years earlier.

In 1675 John was beatified, in 1726 canonised, and in 1926 declared a Doctor of the Church.

John of the Cross was a poet, mystic, theologian and saint. The Church had given him the title of Doctor of the Church, which is confirmation of his learning and holiness. As with other great writer-saints, his writings are distilled from his own life experiences of struggle and prayer. He has written commentaries on his three major poems, and these commentaries tell us much about prayer and, by inference, about his own prayer.

His prose style is different from the rambling, gossipy, conversational style of Teresa, and the gently flowing attractiveness of Julian of Norwich. John's is an interesting mixture of scholastic, logical method and lyricism. At times he rivals the English metaphysical poets with his far-fetched, elaborate conceits and comparisons. He draws heavily on the imagery of the Songs of Songs. It does not always make for easy reading, but when you become at home with his style, he is most rewarding.

As R. H. J. Steuart SJ says in *The Mystical Doctrine of St John of the Cross,* 'To read and study the works of St John of the Cross should not . . . be looked upon as something unusual or freakish, as it is often regarded; nor, on the other hand, as denoting the possession of special and extraordinary grace'.[1]

When I was studying theology in preparation for the priesthood, opinion was divided about the call to be a contemplative in the strict sense, that is, to mystical prayer. Many held that it was for the few, for the elite, while a minority thought all were called but not all responded. More and more writers today are expanding the meaning of mysticism and would say that all are called. John of the Cross remarks that the reason why so few reach union is not because God does not call them, but because they are unwilling to be purified.[2]

John's three major poems are 'The Ascent of Mount Carmel—The Dark Night', 'The Spiritual Canticle' and 'The Living Flame of Love'. These works and the commentaries on them were written during the last fourteen years of his life, when he had attained intellectual and spiritual maturity. The constant theme is the way leading to union with God, and the life of divine union itself.[3]

'The Ascent of Mount Carmel— The Dark Night'

The entire work is composed of four integral parts:

1. A sketch of the Mount.
2. A poem, consisting of eight five-line stanzas, probably written while the saint was confessor to the nuns in Beas, some time between 1579 and 1581. It is an allegory in which a lover sings of her good fortune in having gone out one dark night to be united with her beloved (stanzas 1-5), and then of the wonderful effects of this union (stanzas 6-8).
3. The first part of the commentary, entitled 'The Ascent of Mount Carmel'. It was probably written between 1579 and 1585.
4. The second part of the commentary on the same poem, entitled 'The Dark Night' (1582-85).

'The Ascent of Mount Carmel' 'explains how to reach divine union quickly.'[4] The union sought goes beyond the natural, substantial union with God which we all have by the very fact of existing. God is continually creating and sustaining all of his creation, and in that sense is substantially united with all creatures, without, of course, destroying individual identity. Beyond this natural union is the supernatural union of *likeness*, produced by love. Moving from image (substantial union) to likeness (union of love) is the basic theme of 'The Ascent of Mount Carmel'.

To attain this union of likeness, the soul must travel the purgative or purifying way so that it is purified from disordered love of creatures. John calls the purification process the dark night of the senses and the dark night of the spirit. The dark night of the senses liberates us from being under the power of our senses, whether in prayer or in behaviour. The dark night of the spirit purifies the spiritual faculties or activities of the soul, that is, intellect, memory, will. *The Cloud of Unknowing* advises that those called to contemplative prayer should thrust into the cloud of forgetting all the activities of senses, imagination, intellect, so that the will may gently strive towards God in the cloud of unknowing. John of the Cross gives the name 'nights' to this blocking out of the action of the senses and the powers of the soul. It is not that creatures thwart union with God, but voluntary, inordinate attachment to them does.

The 'Ascent of Mount Carmel' commentary describes in much detail the active purification of the senses and the spirit, that is, the work that must be done by us. The 'Dark Night' commentary deals with the passive purification of senses and spirit, that is, God's activity.

Applying all this teaching to prayer, we see that it directs the movement from meditation, in which we work with our senses and intellect and imagination, to contemplation. The three powers of the soul are taken over by faith, hope and love. The intellect is transcended by faith, so that it knows not by its normal human way, but in a new, though dark, way of faith. The memory is possessed by hope, which frees it from the natural hopes to produce the riches of supernatural hope. The human will is lifted up by divine love to be united to God's will.

And this is the way of knowing through unknowing, the dark way of negation, apophatic mysticism. As we are freed in our behaviour from disordered voluntary appetites, we are being liberated from the pleasure-pain motive to acting only from the love of God. In our living and praying, love is transforming us so that we become what we love.

The first five stanzas of the poem 'The Dark Night' describe the journey. In the first stanza, the dark night is the deprivation of the senses. In the second, the 'darkness' is more obscure than dark, and this is the night of the spirit. Then the night becomes 'glad' and 'guiding'. From twilight to midnight to dawn is the imagery suggested by the journey of the two nights.

The last three stanzas tell of the effects of the union, when the soul is at one with God, though never losing its own identity.

'The Spiritual Canticle'

'The Spiritual Canticle' is a lyrical poem about the love of a soul and Christ, and by implication about the passionate love of the mystic John of the Cross and his beloved. He began his poem in prison in Toledo, writing thirty-one stanzas there from December 1577 to August 1578. The remaining nine stanzas were written later and the commentary still later, at the request of the Carmelite nuns at Beas.

'The Spiritual Canticle' is not a book for beginners but for those already experienced in mystical understanding. There are no clear descriptions of the nights—in fact, the terms are not even used.

John's prologue is careful to allow the reader complete freedom for reflection and prayer. The theme of *The Canticle* is that we can reach a degree of loving intimacy with God in this life that can be described fittingly in the language of married love. We find our God deep within.

This inner searching is the song of the Canticle, and in it the soul walks the traditional purgative, illuminative, unitive ways. Stanzas 1-12 speak of the initial stages of the journey being undertaken by those longing for love. In stanzas 13-21 the soul is illuminated as it is prepared for vision. The union of spiritual marriage is treated in stanzas 22-35, and the poem concludes by describing the Beatific Vision that is attained permanently only after death.

This poem and the commentary on it show us the bridal mysticism of John of the Cross.

When I hear couples during a Marriage Encounter Weekend share the deep, uniting joy of taking on each others' feelings, my thoughts turn to the union between God and the soul that John calls mystical marriage. I sense a likeness.

The 'Spiritual Canticle' is a rich harvest field for our prayer, and many of its lines are memorable.

'The Living Flame of Love'

In this poem of just four stanzas, John of the Cross deals with 'the very intimate and qualified union and transformation of the soul in God'. It is the union with God that is achieved through the likeness of love. 'The Ascent of Mount Carmel' leads us to this highly perfected love within the state of transformation.

Some find it encouraging to begin with 'The Living Flame' so that they may have the vision of what awaits them at the top of the mountain. When the climbing becomes difficult and depressing, the vision of what awaits strengthens their efforts and desires.

The first stanza describes the experience. The living flame is the Holy Spirit, who both wounds and heals. Since the purification has taken place, the Spirit no longer afflicts or wearies or distresses the soul. It is not now oppressive but gentle. The ardent, intense longing for union is expressed by phrases such as 'tear through the veil of this sweet encounter'. The sexual imagery is powerful.

The second stanza deals with the divine cause—the sweet cautery is the Spirit, the gentle hand is the Father, and the delicate touch is the Son. John's mysticism is Trinitarian.

The third and fourth stanzas show the effect of the mystical marriage.

How gently and lovingly
You awake in my heart,
where in secret you dwell alone.

The journey up to the mountain is the journey within, and God is discovered deeply within, dwelling all alone, because the heart has been purified of all rivals for his love.

Abbot Chapman thinks that John of the Cross is for beginners and Teresa for those proficient in prayer, and he says that this was the early view of the Carmelites.[5] This surprised me at first. Now I find that it helps to begin the study of these two great Carmelite doctors of the Church with the poems by John of the Cross, to be warmed by their music and nourished by their truth. Then one may turn to Teresa, and finally come to John's commentaries.

Whatever method is adopted, I am confident that many who are searching for union with God will find John of the Cross 'full of sound spiritual doctrine and well suited to the reader's understanding', as Pius XI said in the bull proclaiming St John of the Cross a Doctor of the Church. He is part of the rich mystical heritage of Christianity.

Reflections

1. Dwell on the distinction between the dark night of the senses and the dark night of the spirit, the active and passive nights. How does this fit into the teaching of *The Cloud of Unknowing*? Have you had prayer experiences where 'nothing happened'? By this phrase did you mean that you had no thoughts? Nevertheless, did you have a sense of deep peace?

2. 'Father, you empowered John of the Cross with a spirit of self-denial and a love of the cross. By following his example, may we come to the eternal vision of your glory. We ask this through our Lord Jesus Christ, your Son, who lives and reigns with you and the Holy Spirit, one God, for ever and ever.' (Mass of St John of the Cross) Do you think this prayer captures the essence of John of the Cross? Could you express in a prayer of your own the appeal John has for you, if you are helped by his poetry?

3. In 'The Living Flame of Love' John speaks of three blind men who can hinder the journey: the spiritual director, the devil, the soul

itself. The importance he places on spiritual direction can be seen from the fact that he devotes fourteen pages to a discussion of the spiritual director, two pages to the devil, and one page to the soul! Read the warnings he gives to spiritual directors. What do you consider to be the most important attribute of a good spiritual director? What is the most harmful? Have you found help from a spiritual director?

4. Read through any of the poems slowly. Pause when a word or a line strikes you and spend time quietly savouring it. You may be helped by turning the passage into a mantra and repeating it during your prayer and during the day. Some examples might be: 'Fired with love's urgent longings'; 'Spirit, living Flame of Love'; 'O guiding night! O night more lovely than the dawn!'; 'Silent music, sounding solitude'.

5. 'I entered into unknowing, and there I remained unknowing, transcending all knowledge.' Compare these words of John with the following quotation from Paul: '. . . Until knowing the love of Christ which is beyond all knowledge, you are filled with the utter fullness of God' (Ephesians 3:18, 19).

6. Jesus often teaches by paradox, and so does John. Compare the following:

   > 'I tell you, most solemnly, unless a wheat grain falls on the ground and dies, it remains only a single grain; but if it dies, it yields a rich harvest. Anyone who loves his life loses it' (John 12:24, 25).

   'To reach satisfaction in all, desire its possession in nothing.'

   'To come to possess all, desire the possession of nothing.'

   Are you challenged or enlightened by this teasing of the intellect? Can you recall an instance in your life when you were enriched by letting go of the desire to possess? If so, recall the experience. How do you feel about it now?

Notes

1. R. H. J. Steuart, *The Mystical Doctrine of St John of the Cross,* Sheed & Ward, London, 1974, p. vii.
2. *Collected Works of St John of the Cross,* ICS Publications, Institute of Carmelite Studies, Washington DC, 1973, p. 604.
3. ibid., p. 33.
4. ibid., p. 68.
5. Dom John Chapman, *Spiritual Letters,* The New Ark Library, Sheed & Ward, London, 1959, pp. 26, 265.

Reading List

Collected Works of St John of the Cross, ICS Publications, Institute of Carmelite Studies, Washington DC, 1973.

St John of the Cross, *The Living Flame of Love,* Simplified Version, by John Venard, OCD, E.J. Dwyer, Sydney, 1990.

St John of the Cross, *The Spiritual Canticle,* Simplified Version, by John Venard, OCD, E.J. Dwyer, Sydney, 1990.

R. H. J. Steuart. *The Mystical Doctrine of St John of the Cross,* Sheed & Ward, London, 1974.

Thomas H. Green SJ, *When the Well Runs Dry,* Ave Maria Press, Notre Dame, Indiana, 1979.

18.

St Teresa of Jesus

Doctor of the Church

St Teresa was born in 1515 and entered the Carmelite Convent of the Incarnation when she was twenty-one. On 3 November 1537 she was professed. Falling seriously ill, she returned home and was believed to have died. She describes coming to and finding preparations underway for her burial. By 1540, however, she was cured and returned to the convent. Her *Life* tells of intense suffering and the favours she received from God.

During Lent in 1554, when she was praying before an Ecce Homo statue (a popular image of the thorn-crowned head of Christ), she experienced what is called her second conversion. Here is how she describes what happened:

> I felt so keenly aware of how poorly I thanked Him for those wounds that, it seems to me, my heart broke. Beseeching Him to strengthen me once and for all that I might not offend Him, I threw myself down before Him with the greatest outpouring of tears.[1]

This was the call to a true mystical journey. It was a second conversion as her heart, up to this time divided between God and the world, and trapped by mediocrity, was freed as she began her surrender to God.

In 1560 St Teresa and a few friends decided to found a Carmelite Convent in conformity with the Primitive Rule of the Order. Despite her ill health she embarked on the Reform. She met John of the Cross in 1567, when he was aged twenty-five and considering joining the Carthusians, and she was fifty-two and seeking to enlist his help with the Reform. This he gave and he also helped her with her mystical journey. Somehow she found time to found eighteen convents and to write books that have become classics of spirituality.

Teresa died in 1582 and was canonised in 1622 along with Isidore, Ignatius Loyola, Francis Xavier and Philip Neri. Paul VI declared her Doctor of the Church in 1970.

Like Ignatius, Teresa belongs to the kataphatic tradition of mysticism. She represents an interesting contrast with John of the Cross and *The Cloud.* Christian mysticism is indeed wide-ranging.

Teresa has bequeathed to us three outstanding books and these are treasures for all, beginners in prayer as well as those mystically gifted. The first is *The Life,* the second *The Way of Perfection,* and, finally, her masterpiece, *The Interior Castle.* In addition we have *Thoughts in the House of God, Spiritual Testimonies, Soliloquies, Meditations on the Song of Songs* and many letters.

'The Life'

Teresa was forty-seven when, under obedience to her confessors, she wrote the *Book of her Life.* This is not strictly an autobiography, although it is filled with autobiographical details, nor is it an intimate diary. What she mainly deals with are the supernatural realities of the interior life, and the way God helped her to keep praying 'even though I continued to associate with the world.'[2] It really is a tribute to 'The Mercies of God', who healed her heart, which was divided between the world and God.

The first ten chapters, describe her journey, interspersed with such beautiful gems about prayer as this:

> Though we are always in the presence of God, it seems to me the manner is different with those who practise prayer. For they are aware that he is looking at them. With others it can happen that several days pass without their recalling that God sees them.[3]

She urges the practice of mental prayer: 'For mental prayer in my opinion is nothing less than an intimate sharing between friends; it means taking time frequently to be alone with him who we know loves us.'[4]

Teresa is not writing for publication but for her own sisters, so we find her very open in sharing her own prayer life. She is more open about her own prayer than anybody else whose works I have read, and this trust makes her very helpful and disarmingly attractive. So she will tell us that her prayer was not always easy and at times she was more anxious for the hour to end than to pray, 'more anxious to listen for the striking of the clock than to attend to other good things.'[5] This is an experience that all can relate to.

She notes how she prays:

> This is the method of prayer I then used: since I could not reflect discursively with the intellect, I strove to picture Christ within me, and it did me greater good—in my opinion—to picture Him in those scenes where I saw Him more alone. It seemed to me that living alone and afflicted, as a person in need, He had to accept me. I had many simple thoughts like these.[6]

Ignatius presents a discursive use of the imagination for scriptural contemplation. In his 'Composition', 'Seeing the Place' and 'Application of Senses', in the *Spiritual Exercises* he recommends fixing the imagination on the scene. It's like freezing the frame of a film. Teresa is helped by this freezing, this continued focus on the frame, a single moment rather than ranging far and wide through the whole scene. Chapter 9, where this practice is set forth, is filled with great helps for prayer.

The sacred humanity of Jesus and his Passion are features of the above work and they continue to dominate her prayer life. In the account Teresa is giving of her spiritual journey she is letting us see how she, like Ignatius and John, experiences the purgative, purifying 'Night of the Senses and Spirit'. In chapter 23, she describes the fears she had that the devil was deceiving her and how St Francis Borgia SJ reassured her and guided her. This was in 1554, the year after her second conversion.

Chapter 11 begins a long digression that continues until chapter 22. This is Teresa's famous four waters image for explaining growth in prayer. She likens the way the Lord leads the soul in prayer to four ways of watering a garden.

First of all, 'His Majesty pulls up the weeds and plants good seeds'. This preparation takes place before the soul is determined 'to practise prayer and has begun to make use of it'. Teresa is a good guide in prayer for our times because she appreciates the importance of self-denial as a prerequisite for growth in prayer. Today this is not always accepted.

Using the analogy of watering a garden, she describes four degrees of prayer.

The first way to water the garden is by drawing water by hand from a well. 'Beginners in prayer, we can say, are those who draw water from the well.' They devote much effort to recollection, to working with the intellect, and to struggling with distractions. These are people who practise meditation. They should keep Christ present to them, and 'speak with and delight in him and not wear themselves out composing syllogisms; rather they should show him their needs'.

Teresa understands well that meditation should move us to acts of the will, or as we tend to say today, move us from the mind to the heart. All her teaching here is most helpful for those who wish to progress. She was at this stage herself for many years and writes out of her own experiences. Above all, she says, we must wait on God to call us into the next stage.

The second way to water the garden is by means of a water wheel and aqueducts. This is the prayer of quiet. The intellect, the memory and imagination are not helpful, although they are not lost, nor are they asleep. Only the will is held by God's love. The prayer is not tiring, but filled with joy. There is growth in virtue and the craving for earthly things is lessened.

Teresa says that many reach this prayer of quiet, but few pass beyond it. She reminds us again of the need to keep purifying our reflections, and not leave discursive meditation completely behind. We are to guard against deceptions by being determined to follow the way of the cross and not to desire consolations.

The third way the garden is watered is with water flowing from a river or stream. This is the prayer of the 'sleep of the faculties'. The faculties neither fail to function entirely nor understand how they function. Teresa says they are asleep. There is less labour, though some is needed to direct the flow. The Lord becomes gardener, and does practically everything. Consolation is greater and there is a longing for God alone. The will is now at rest, though not fully united with God.

Teresa experienced this prayer for five or six years and says, 'I didn't understand it'.

Water may also be provided by a fourth means, a great deal of rain. The soul rejoices and the faculties are united with God. This is the highest form of union that Teresa experienced when she was writing her *Life*. She struggles to describe this, using the image of the fire burning and flaming, as does John of the Cross in *The Living Flame of Love*. Only after she met John of the Cross was she raised to mystical marriage.

These twelve chapters in the *Life* (11–22) are a beautiful treatise on prayer, and my brief presentation, like any summary, will be helpful only if it leads to reading what the saint herself has written.

'The Way of Perfection'

Father Banez OP, Teresa's confessor, did not feel at ease about the nuns and others reading *The Life,* because he feared that the accounts of mystical prayer might mislead some. But the nuns wanted to read it, so Banez agreed that Teresa should write 'some things about prayer'. Thus we have *The Way of Perfection,* completed probably in 1569.

It is full of simple, practical advice. Teresa's reflection on the 'Our Father' is a beautiful introduction to the prayer of recollection. As always, prayer to the sacred humanity of Jesus and about his Passion is central to her teaching. Her principle is the very simple one: Pray as you can.

'The Interior Castle'

Teresa was sixty-two when she wrote her masterpiece, *The Interior Castle*. Incredibly, it took her three months. She was more experienced in mystical prayer than when she wrote her *Life* and *The Way*.

Just as she used the analogy of watering a garden to explain the four degrees of prayer, in *The Interior Castle* she used the image of a castle with circular tiers of rooms. One enters the outer rooms and moves through tier after tier until one comes to the deepest centre where His Majesty dwells, the beautiful Jewel deep within. Passing through circle after circle is like peeling off outer layers to get to the kernel.

Teresa sees prayer growth and spiritual growth as a journey inwards, whereas John of the Cross sees it as a journey upwards to the Mount, and Ignatius uses the model of four progressive stages that he calls 'weeks'. All three seek transforming union by conversion, conformation and transformation. Teresa and Ignatius present the kataphatic way, the affirmative way, while John uses the apophatic, negative way of unknowing. Teresa's approach is more experimental than speculative, more descriptive than deductive. She thus differs from John, the trained scholastic theologian. On the other hand, neither Ignatius nor Teresa has the wonderful poetic gifts of John.

There are seven mansions (dwelling places) in Teresa's interior castle. Each one of these mansions should be understood to contain many rooms. The first three mansions represent what is called acquired contemplation. This is ordinary prayer, not mystical prayer. The fourth, fifth, sixth and seventh mansions deal with mystical prayer, infused contemplation and extraordinary prayer. The castle is the place of intimate friendship with God. For Teresa, as for Ignatius, intimacy with our God comes through the humanity of Jesus. God is ever present in the soul and *The Interior Castle* teaches how we can make the inner journey to be united with him in the seventh mansion.

Each mansion indicates how we should be living, as well as offering a way of praying that is in harmony with our way of life. With Teresa, praying, loving and living go hand in hand.

We can apply the classical, traditional ways of the spiritual life to the journey through the castle. The first, second and third mansions are the purgative way, the fourth the illuminative way, and the fifth, sixth and seventh the unitive way.

To walk through these mansions is a rewarding journey. The first mansion is important for progress, as here we gain self-knowledge, leading us to true humility. We are warned against always looking at our weaknesses, and exhorted to look at Christ. Prayer is mainly vocal prayer. I am reminded of *The Cloud,* the opening experiences of the *Spiritual Exercises,* and the Encounter with self-talk in the Marriage Encounter Weekend.

The second mansion refers us to chapters XI–XIII of *The Way of Perfection.* Teresa is encouraging: 'All that the beginner in prayer has to do—and you must not forget this, for it is very important—is to labour and be resolute and prepare himself with all possible diligence to bring his will into conformity with the will of God.'[7] It is a time of struggle, but we are urged not to abandon prayer, which has moved to meditation and which develops the virtues. Prayer is consoling.

The third mansion stresses the importance of humility, detachment, confident trust in God. Experiences of aridity and dryness purify the soul. Prayer is simpler: simple regard—just looking—becomes the usual form.

The fourth mansion marks the beginning of mystical prayer; infused contemplation begins to succeed the acquired contemplation. 'To grow in prayer do not think much, love much. Love is in the will, not in the mind.' We are reminded of *The Cloud of Unknowing*. The graces of this mansion referred to as 'spiritual consolations' are identified with the prayer of quiet or the second water of the *Life*.

The fifth mansion speaks of the prayer of union as the human will is united with the will of God. This is the introduction to the prayer of the sixth and seventh mansions. In her description of this prayer, Teresa uses the famous image of the silk worms and the cocoons.

Eleven chapters are devoted to the sixth mansion. It is the prayer of conforming union, and Teresa calls it espousals. She discusses phenomena associated with mysticism, such as locutions, trances, raptures, ecstacy and visions. Then suddenly in chapter VIII, she writes beautifully about the contemplation of Jesus and his Passion. For her, contemplation is the simple gaze on Christ in the mystery, not the discursive use of the intellect or the imagination.

The seventh mansion is the spiritual marriage, a second Heaven. The spiritual marriage, unlike the spiritual betrothal of the sixth mansion, lasts, and the soul never loses its peace. This is the prayer of transforming union.

There is a final warning not to build upon foundations of prayer and contemplation alone, but on true humility.

Teresa differs from Ignatius in that hers is a bridal mysticism, while his is a mysticism of service. Both are explicitly Christ-centred in their prayer, more openly so than the author of *The Cloud* and John of the Cross. All are ecclesial, in their full allegiance to the Church. In this they are a counter to some contemporary tendencies to set mysticism at odds with the Church. Harvey Egan writes:

> The Christian Faith is an Easter Faith. Among the classical Christian mystics, perhaps St Teresa has the best explicit grasp of this key point. The resurrection-centeredness of her mysticism and spirituality needs strong emphasis today.[8]

The teaching of Teresa on prayer inspires us with strong hope, so important in a contemporary world tempted to despair. Her doctrine is likewise useful for the many who are seeking contemplation. She is so sensible, ordinary, down to earth, good-humoured, that she anchors prayer among 'the pots and the pans', in true humility, and guards against the errors of pseudo-mystical flights. Significantly, during her account of the espousals in the sixth mansion, she returns to praise the practice of contemplating the humanity of Jesus. Sharing her own experience of praying the prayer of simple regard will help many who are moving from meditation (discursive use of intellect), scriptural contemplation (discursive use of the imagination) to simply dwelling on a scriptural scene, with little work by the senses, intellect or memory.

I am sure, too, that all of us who support the modern movement to redress the oppression of women in the world and the Church will applaud Paul VI's decision to make Teresa a Doctor of the Church. Perhaps he was amused and influenced by her delightful attack on male chauvinism in *The Way of Perfection.*

Above all else, what makes St Teresa of Jesus a wonderful prayer companion is her freedom to follow where the Spirit is leading in ways of prayer. So pray the way that suits you. All that ultimately matters is that you encounter God.

Reflections

1. Ruth Burrows links the biblical periods to the journey into the interior of the castle:

Old Testament Preparation for visitation of God	Mansions 1,2,3
The era of Jesus Entering the paschal mystery	Mansions 4,5,6
The era of the Spirit Risen life	Mansion 7

   Ponder this linkage. Does it help you in your understanding of Teresa's teaching on prayer? Is your own prayer helped?

2. Reflect on the images used by Teresa to instruct us about prayer: the watering of the garden, the silkworms and the cocoons, the castle. Which do you find the most helpful? Imagine you are helping children in their prayer growth; which image would you prefer? Try a fantasy exercise: first imagine you are the gardener, or the garden, then imagine you are the water. Construct your own fantasy exercise for the other two images.

3. Both Teresa and Julian of Norwich enter their mystical journey by reflecting on the Cross of Jesus. Read the two accounts and compare. Which appeals most to you?

4. Jung speaks of the inner journey people take to discover their true self. He says that this is normally a mid-life experience. Teresa struggled for about eighteen years with her mediocrity, her ambivalence towards God and the world, before her experience with the Ecce Homo statue at the age of thirty-nine. Compare the psychological path taken by Jung and the spiritual path of Teresa. Jung advises taking off your masks. What are your masks? Teresa advocates the freedom to pray as you can. How free are you to follow the Spirit in your prayer?

5. In *The Way* (chapters 28 and 29) Teresa describes how she was freed from error in her prayer through the advice given by St Francis Borgia and the earlier confessors. What did she learn from this? (See also *The Interior Castle,* the sixth mansion.) Are you able to talk about your prayer experiences to anyone? Or do you talk just about your problems? Have you been able to find a helpful spiritual director? Do you think God might be calling you to be a prayer companion to others?

Notes

1. *Life,* p. 71, *Collected Works of St Teresa of Avila,* vol. I, ICS Publications, Institute of Carmelite Studies, Washington DC, 1980.
2. ibid., p. 66.
3. ibid., p. 66.
4. ibid., p. 67.
5. ibid., p. 68.
6. ibid., p. 71.
7. *Collected Works,* vol. II, p. 301.
8. Harvey D. Egan SJ, *Christian Mysticism,* Pueblo Publishing Company, New York, 1984, p. 162.

Reading List

Collected Works of St Teresa of Avila, 3 volumes, ICS Publications, Institute of Carmelite Studies, Washington DC, 1980.

Ruth Burrows, *Interior Castle Explored,* Sheed & Ward/Veritas Publications, London & Dublin, 1982.

Praying with Saint Teresa, Compiled by Battistina Capalbo, SPCK, London, 1988.

19.

St Francis de Sales

'Jogging Along'

Frances de Sales is a most lovable saint. He was a nobleman of Savoy, but much influenced by France. Of him, Henry IV, King of France, said:

> A rare bird indeed; devout, learned and a gentleman into the bargain . . . He does not know the art of flattery; his mind is too sincere for that . . . He is the person most capable of restoring the ecclesiastical order to its first splendour. He is gentle, good and humble—deeply pious but without useless scruples.[1]

The king of France was just one of the many whom Francis won over during his life. Since his death his two famous books *Introduction to the Devout Life* and *Treatise on the Love of God* have continued to charm and instruct. Both are Christian classics.

Francis de Sales was born in 1567. Ignatius Loyola had died eleven years before, Teresa and John of the Cross were busy with the Reform, Philip Neri was delighting Rome. Like John of the Cross, Francis was educated by the Jesuits, who prepared him at Padua for studies at the University of Paris. Father Antonio Possevino SJ gave him spiritual guidance during those important years of his formation at Padua.

During his stay in Paris he was sorely tempted to despair as he brooded over the many who, if the Calvinists were to be believed, were destined to be damned. This was a time of great anguish, a veritable dark night. Francis was safeguarded from turning in on himself with self-pity, however. God led him to the Lady Chapel where he prayed: 'Whatever happens, O Lord, you hold everything in your hands, and all your ways are just and true'.

By chance he saw a prayer card of St Bernard's famous *Memorare*, the prayer that begins 'Remember, O most gracious Virgin Mary . . .'. Suddenly he found peace as he turned also to Mary. Later he would write: 'When [meditations] finish in fear, they are dangerous . . . God is not so terrible for those who love Him . . . He asks little of us because He knows how little we have'.[2] This experience freed Francis from the false and frightening image of a punishing God, enabling him to love a God who loved him unconditionally.

When he had completed his university course in Paris, he returned home, but soon he went to Padua to take out a doctorate of law. Here he was again helped by the Jesuit, Antonio Possevino, who remained a lifelong friend. Francis fell victim to an epidemic that swept through Padua and was believed to be dying. After receiving the Last Sacraments from Father Possevino, however, he slowly began to recover. God seems to repeat himself—Julian of Norwich, Teresa of Jesus, Ignatius Loyola all travelled the same road.

In 1593 Francis was ordained priest and, after a difficult mission to make converts from Calvinism, he was consecrated Bishop of Geneva in 1602. He was a dedicated pastor who resisted efforts to give him higher honours. 'Sire,' he said to Henry IV, 'I have married a poor wife and I cannot desert her for a richer one'.[3]

Two years later his beautiful friendship with Jane Frances de Chantal began, and with her in 1610 he founded the Visitation Order. *Introduction to the Devout Life* was published in 1608 and *A Treatise on the Love of God* in 1616.

Worn out by his busy labours and ill health, Francis died at Lyons in 1622, only fifty-five years of age. He was canonised in 1665, proclaimed Doctor of the Church in 1877 and Patron of Journalists in 1923—many were the honours bestowed on this simple, lovable saint who during his life sought to escape honours.

The great reform movement within the Church in the sixteenth century directed its efforts against the triple scandals of ignorance, avarice and immorality among the clergy. We have seen something of the Spanish saints. St Philip Neri, St Charles Borromeo, St Vincent de Paul, St Francis de Sales, and St Jane Frances de Chantal were just some of the others whose lives gave witness to the reforming power of the Spirit of God in the Church.

Francis was well educated in humanism and in theology. He was influenced in his spirituality by the Jesuits, by Madame Acarie (1566–1618), by St Teresa of Jesus (whose writings were translated into French in 1601), by the mystical graces of St Jane Frances de Chantal, by St Charles Borromeo and by the Council of Trent.

His influence was powerful and widespread. Preaching, catechising, caring for the poor, and for children—these services were all part of his busy day. His writing, too, was a rich apostolate. In addition to his two famous books, which made monastic spirituality and prayer available to all, there was a busy apostolate of letterwriting and spiritual guidance. He was the spiritual guide of Jane Frances de Chantal, with whom he co-founded the Visitation Order.

His way of life was marked by spiritual and actual poverty and a deep fidelity to prayer. Francis mixed easily in the French Court and enjoyed a warm friendship with Henry IV. He was no great orator, but he spoke from the heart, with Christian simplicity. In founding the Visitation Order he broke with tradition, as the nuns wore lay dress and were not enclosed. Like Ignatius, he moved monastic spirituality into the marketplace, an example followed by Tenison Woods and Mary MacKillop about three hundred years later, when they founded the Sisters of St Joseph in Australia.

St Francis de Sales was, and through his books still is, a good spiritual director. His guidance was firm, sure and kindly, and often couched in a friendly sense of humour. He did not take himself too seriously, whether at the Court of France, among the peasants at Chablais, or with the Calvinists in Geneva. 'One jogs along as one can!' he said.

When he was consecrating a cemetery and it rained, the Calvinists taunted him with the gibe that God was punishing him. 'No,' he replied, 'the devil is angry at being driven out'.

A freedom to flow along with God characterised his guidance, as we see in the growth of the Visitation Order, in his own openness to contemplation, in his ability to find God all around him and to use his keen powers of observation to illustrate his teaching. He took examples from everywhere.

Modern psychologists would applaud the advice he gave to one who was depressed:

> If you are attacked by sadness or bitterness, lift up your heart to God; then seek relaxation. Hold a cheerful conversation, go out for a walk, read one of your favourite books, sing a holy song. In this way you will gradually ward off spiritual melancholy.

And again: 'Beware of all brooding introspection: God's Spirit cannot dwell in a soul forever occupied in self-analysis.'

How beautifully he helps those over-concerned about their own perfection, as they seek to placate a punishing God, or to please the God of the Hundred Per Cent!

'Introduction to the Devout Life'

The *Introduction* was first published in 1608 and the final revised edition appeared in 1619. It was designed to help the ordinary lay person towards spiritual perfection, a revolutionary concept then, which well illustrates the modernity of St Francis. He believed that the strongest counter to Calvinism was not only the teaching of correct doctrine, but also the nourishing of a sincere and fervent interior life.

There are five parts to *The Devout Life*. It begins by addressing an imaginary reader he calls Philothea, to whom he gives the true meaning of devotion:

> True, living devotion, Philothea, presupposes the love of God; and hence it is nothing else than the love of God . . . In short, devotion is nothing else than the spiritual agility and vivacity which charity works in us, or we work by her aid, with alacrity and affection.[4]

This call to integrate the love of God, our Christianity, into our lives is an invitation not only to the privileged few in the cloister, but to all.

What follows is a simple, systematic programme that has echoes of Ignatius, Teresa and John of the Cross, with its stress on purgation from sin and the effects of sin. Ten meditations are presented in this opening part. Instructions on prayer, the sacraments, the virtues, resistance to the temptations that attack the soul striving for perfection, and advice on annual renewal from the other four parts. Francis' style is interesting and simple. It is not surprising that *The Devout Life* continues to be a Christian classic of spirituality, because it is still most relevant, a fundamental, sensible handbook for the journey to wholeness.

Treatise on the Love of God

The *Treatise on the Love of God* was published in 1616. It is a sequel to *The Devout Life*, and particularly in its treatment of meditation, contemplation and mystical prayer, goes far beyond it. At first Francis was reserved about contemplative prayer, but he was opened up to it by Jane Frances de Chantal, Madame Acarie and Blessed Mary of the Incarnation, as well as by his reading of the mystics. His role as spiritual director to the nuns of the Visitation Order also widened his horizons.

As a result, in the *Treatise* we have instruction on prayer that for its sound doctrine and clear presentation can be placed in the hands of all. Those who use meditation and conceptual images in their prayer will find clear understanding and guidance, as will those who find that their prayer had become simpler and that images and thoughts play little part in it. Francis writes beautifully on the different stages in the growth of prayer, clearly influenced by St Teresa of Jesus.

I found book VI very rewarding for its treatment of meditation and contemplation. Consider the following quotations, for example:

> Contemplation is simply the mind's loving, unmixed, permanent attention to the things of God.[5]

> Desire to obtain divine love causes us to meditate, but the love obtained causes us to contemplate.[6]

> In summary, meditation is the mother of the love but contemplation is its daughter. For this reason I have called contemplation a loving attention, since children are named after their fathers, not fathers after children.[7]

> Love urges the eyes continually to look more attentively at the loved beauty, while sight forces the heart to love it ever more ardently.[8]

Loving and contemplating are mutually nourishing.

Good spiritual director that he is, Francis points out the big difference between being occupied with God who gives us contentment, and concerning ourselves with the contentment God gives us.[9] Seek the God of consolations, he says, not the consolations of God, and focus on God, not the repose, not the self.

> A man who has scarcely any love for God has scarcely any more hatred for sin. Love is the first—in fact, the very principle and source—of all the passions.[10]

. . . when a man has more light in his intellect for wondering about God than warmth in his will to love him, he ought to be on guard.[11]

A lifting up in prayer [ecstasy] without a lifting up in living is not from God.[12]

The book is filled with incisive, sensible advice like this. That is why St Francis de Sales is a safe guide for pilgrims of the interior life.

Perhaps the most charming feature of Francis was his deeply affectionate character. He made friends with many. His account to Jane Frances of his mother's death is moving:

It was one of the most beautiful deaths I have ever witnessed. And I must tell you that I had the courage to give her the last blessing, to close her eyes and to give her the last kiss of peace as she died. Only after that did my heart melt, and I wept for so good a mother more than I have ever done since I became a churchman. But my sorrow was, thanks be to God, without any spiritual bitterness. This is all that happened.[13]

How much this account tells us of the deeply loving man who won so many friends!

The love Francis had for Jane Frances de Chantal and her love for him illustrate how comfortable both were with deep human love. Their story is a powerful witness to a modern world confused about love, sex and the mystery of a deep loving between celibate men and women. The letter he wrote to Jane Frances about his mother's death reveals not only the love he had for his mother, but also his love for Jane Frances:

You would wish to know how this good woman has ended her days. Here is a little account of it, for it is to you that I speak—you to whom I have given the place of my mother in my Memento in the Mass without taking away the place you had in it before, for I could not omit this, so close do I hold you in my heart. You are the first and last in it.[14]

Francis was able to talk freely with Jane, as he did, for example, about the difficulties of pastoral visitation:

Don't be jealous, I tell you again. You are not the only one to have a cross to carry. Yes, since you desire it, I must start speaking of myself from this aspect. After all it is the truth; yesterday, all day and all night, I had to carry a cross like yours, not in my head but in my heart . . . It is true that yesterday I felt my will to be so feeble that a mite would have been strong enough to crush it.[15]

Again he ends news about his mission by saying, 'I tell you all this because my heart cannot hide anything from yours. It cannot be different or other than yours—but just one with yours.'[16]

Their meeting seemed divinely arranged. Each, separately, had visions of the other. Jane Frances was happily married for eight years, with four surviving children, when her husband was accidentally shot by a friend. Before he died, he said that he wanted no blame attached to his friend, but Jane Frances found that hard. Francis gave her wise advice, and also brought her through her deep grieving to begin living again. His spiritual direction of Jane Frances freed her and led her into mystical prayer. In turn she freed him so that he could write so helpfully in the *Treatise on the Love of God* about the different stages of contemplation.

Towards the end of his life, Jane Frances spoke of her concern about a difficult journey he made over the Alps.

> Overcome by all this, he crossed the mountains affected by unbearable pain and inconvenience, because of the piles from which he was suffering and the consequent loss of blood. So ill was he that the attendants did not think that he would live to see his home again.[17]

Their last conversation on earth was eighteen years after they had first met at Dijon.

The driving force in the life of St Francis de Sales was love, human and divine. 'Love will shake the walls of Geneva,' he said, 'not gunpowder'. He was twice close to death, experienced severe temptations against faith and suffered much from poor circulation, but he abandoned himself to God's love.

He was convinced that love conquers all, not fear. Love was central to his life and is central to the message he passed on to us.

Reflections

1. Julian of Norwich said that love is God's meaning and spoke of being enfolded with love. Compare her with St Francis de Sales. Who do you think helps you more in your prayer?

2. Reflect on the deep, non-possessive love between Francis and Jane Frances de Chantal. Consider the challenges involved in celibate loving and the rewards. In what way is their love a witness to our times?

3. 'Love seeks that which it has already found, not to have it but to have it forever.'[18]

   'We become what we love, like the mirror which takes in the countenance without diminishing the looker.'[19]

   Reflect on these two quotations from the *Treatise*. Can you recall an experience of deepening your love for a person by continuing to seek in love? As you stay with the memory, be aware of your feelings. In what sense have you become what you love? Have you diminished the other person? What about your own experience of being loved? Do you find the two statements by Francis are verified?

4. 'Whatever happens, Lord, may I at least love you in this life if I cannot love you in eternity since no one may praise you in hell. May I at least make use of every moment of my short life on earth to love you.'[20]

   'He who preaches with love is preaching well enough against heretics even though he does not utter a word against them.'[21]

   In his theology Francis was a man of his times. Are you at ease with the above statements? If not, why not? Do you see a tension between his theology and the centrality of love in his life? In your own life do you ever experience such a tension? Which do you think comes first, theology or love? Do you know of cases where this choice is very real to people?

5. Does your own prayer grow out of theology, or out of love, or both?

Notes

1. Michael de la Bedoyere, *Francis de Sales*, Harper & Brothers, New York, 1960, p. 91.
2. ibid., p. 28.
3. ibid., p. 92.
4. St Francis de Sales, *Introduction to The Devout Life*, translated by Monsignor Ryan, Longman, Green & Company, London, 1953, p. 2.
5. St Francis de Sales, *Treatise on the Love of God*, translated by Rt Rev John K. Ryan, 2 volumes, Tan Books, Rockford, Illinois, 1975, vol. 1, p. 275.
6. ibid., p. 275.
7. ibid., p. 276.

8. ibid., p. 276.
9. ibid., p. 294.
10. ibid., p. 303.
11. ibid., vol. II, p. 30.
12. ibid., p. 33.
13. Michael de la Bedoyere, *Francis de Sales,* p. 181.
14. ibid., p. 180.
15. ibid., p. 132.
16. ibid., p. 132.
17. ibid., p. 235.
18. *Treatise on the Love of God,* vol. I, p. 242.
19. ibid., p. 235.
20. Michael de la Bedoyere, *Francis de Sales,* p. 26.
21. ibid., p. 93.

Reading List

Michael de la Bedoyere, *Francis de Sales,* Harper & Brothers, New York, 1960.

St Francis de Sales, *Introduction to the Devout Life,* Longmans, Green & Company, London, 1953.

St Francis de Sales, *Treatise on the Love of God,* 2 volumes, Tan Books, Rockford, Illinois, 1975.

20.

Jean-Pierre de Caussade

Sacrament of the Present Moment

Jean-Pierre de Caussade was born in 1675 and became a Jesuit novice in 1693. He was ordained a priest in 1704, and took his final vows in 1708. His ministry began with teaching Greek and Latin, then philosophy and theology. After that, he was preacher and confessor in many places. In 1729 he became director of the Visitation nuns, and for the last five years of his life he was director of theological students at Toulouse. In his book, *On Prayer according to Bossuet,* published in 1741, he defended true mysticism. He died in 1751.

In 1861, Father Ramière gathered the retreat notes and letters of Jean-Pierre and published them under the title of *Abandonment to Divine Providence,* which became a perennially popular spiritual book. It was first published in France in 1861, and has gone through many editions and translations. A recent translator has changed the well-known English title to *The Joy of Full Surrender,* arguing that it is difficult to convey the full meaning of the French word *abandon* without being negative or fatalistic. To bring out the very positive hope in Jean-Pierre's message, Hal M. Helms has recently presented a revised translation; unfortunately it is marred by bad misprints. Kitty Muggeridge has recently translated two books of Jean-Pierre's writings, *The Sacrament of the Present Moment* and *Spiritual Letters of Jean-Pierre de Caussade.*

As is to be expected, since he was a Jesuit, Jean-Pierre was influenced by Ignatius Loyola and the *Spiritual Exercises.* Ignatian 'indifference', which means being completely ready to do whatever God wants and which is, therefore, a positive attachment to God, is echoed in concepts of abandonment. Finding God in all things and the 'Contemplation for Attaining Divine Love' are also caught up in Jean-Pierre's teaching about the sacrament of the present moment, and the journey of the faith-search.

St Francis de Sales was a powerful formative influence. Francis had died in 1622, fifty-three years before Jean-Pierre was born, but his teaching lived on. Being spiritual director to the nuns of the Visitation Order would have made Jean-Pierre very familiar with the devout Doctor's legacy. Bossuet led him to Francis. The spirituality of the heart, which we find in the teaching of Francis, his mildness, gentleness and confidence in God, all made their mark on his disciple.

So also did the renunciation taught by John of the Cross. *The Ascent of Mount Carmel* speaks of God being present to us in the prayer of faith, reforming, illuminating and transforming. This thought is to be found in *The Sacrament of the Present Moment,* too.

As Archbishop Goodier points out, Jean-Pierre de Caussade lived in a time when Jansenism and quietism had made the spiritual writers of France nervous. Jansenism froze the heart, but the teaching of *Abandonment to Divine Providence* was about the God who loves us and frees us, as St Francis de Sales taught, when he was freed from fears of a punishing God.

Quietism in its widest sense can mean the tendency to exaggerate the role of passivity and repose in the spiritual life. Jean-Pierre, like Ignatius, John of the Cross and Teresa, taught that in prayer we are not to be completely passive. Hence he reassured many who were handicapped in their prayer journey because they were ignorant of true mysticism and so afraid of being deluded.

'Abandonment to Divine Providence'

Jean-Pierre's teaching on abandonment is, as we have seen, inspired by the concept of indifference, which is presented in the 'Principle and Foundation' exercise of the *Spiritual Exercises,* developed and explored throughout the 'four-week journey', culminating in the 'Take, O Lord, and Receive' prayer in the 'Contemplation for Attaining Divine Love'. The self-abandonment Jean-Pierre proposes goes further than resignation or toleration or conformity. Such responses do not capture the positive movement of an acceptance that embraces the situation presented. Ascetic self-denial, renunciation of self, self-love, self-will—which all result from the purification of the 'Ascent of Mount Carmel' and the first week of the *Exercises*—are assumed. Acceptance of the will of God is the duty of every Christian, and this is shown by obeying the laws of God and the Church. Jean-Pierre calls this acceptance 'active fidelity'.

Passive fidelity (faithfulness), on the other hand, consists in the loving acceptance of all that God sends us each moment, and so it ranges far beyond laws. This passive fidelity is not the helplessness of fatalism, and neither is it a stoical resignation or an abject abdication of one's will. Nor is it the hopelessness of Dante's warning over the gateway of Hell—'Abandon hope all you who enter here', where the situation is overpowering. It is at a far remove from despair and is an acceptance with the full surrender of one's will moved by faith, hope and love.

Jean-Pierre takes care to safeguard his teaching from any charge of quietism, which would have God alone active: 'It is foolish to picture any kind of self-surrender in which all personal activity is excluded'.[1]

I meet people who seem to operate from either end of the spectrum. Some are in despair and have given up all hope. Others expect God to come with a magic wand, while they sit back doing nothing. Both types have in common the fact that they do nothing. A correct understanding of Jean-Pierre's words is a help here.

His concept of abandonment is similar to a swimmer's trusting surrender to the water when floating. It is like throwing oneself onto the mercy of a loving parent, partner or friend. Such surrender is done with confidence and trust.

In book II, Jean-Pierre moves from the virtue of self-abandonment to the state of being surrendered to God's will. When gifted with this state, 'the soul lives in God . . . and God lives in the soul'.[2] 'When God lives in the soul, it should surrender itself completely to his providence.' The influence of *The Cloud* and *The Dark Night* are evident here, as the soul leaves everything else to be guided by God alone, and everything is accepted as God's will and presence.

> The state of full surrender is a certain combination of faith, hope and love in one single action which unites the soul to God and His will. United, these three virtues together form but a single act, the raising of the heart to God and surrender to His divine work.[3]

God is seen by faith, hoped for by hope, and loved by love. All is entrusted to him, spiritual and material concerns, so that one rests trustfully in his love.

Writing to Sister Anne-Marguerite Boudet, Jean-Pierre describes fully what he means by this state of self-surrender, which God alone can give, and by which he invites us 'to remain before him in silence and a humble recollection'.[4] He then gives three indications 'which enable us in the long run to see the results of the Divine action and the changes produced in the heart'. These are

(1) A holy indifference like a sort of stupidity in reference to the things of this world.
(2) A depth of peace such that you no longer worry about anything at the bottom of your soul, not even over your own imperfections and faults, and still less over those of others.
(3) A certain zest for God and the things of God, a sort of hunger and thirst for justice i.e. for virtue, piety and all perfection. This hunger which is very keenly felt is, however, exempt from hurry and anxiety; it leads us to wish all that God wishes and nothing more, to bless him in our spiritual poverty as in our spiritual abundance.[5]

The letters show what a fine spiritual director Jean-Pierre de Caussade was.

'The Sacrament of the Present Moment'

Dom John Chapman makes twenty-one references to Jean-Pierre de Caussade in his *Spiritual Letters* and he says that in the last decade or so of his life he obtained more help from Père de Caussade, and especially from his letters, than from any writer since St Francis de Sales.[6] The 'sacrament of the present moment', he writes, is

> an illuminating phrase which, by its startling originality, brings home the value of his teaching that God reveals his will to us under the outward and visible circumstances of our lives, in much the same way as he imparts his graces to us under the tangible symbols of his sacraments . . .[7]

Each moment is God coming to us. Just as the sacraments bring us God's love, so each moment, each 'now' event, is like a sacrament because it brings us God's love.

> The present moment is always filled with infinite treasure. It contains more than you have the capacity to hold. Faith is the measure of these

> treasures; according to your faith you will receive. Love also is the measure. The more the heart loves, the more it desires, and the more it will receive.[8]

Jean-Pierre compares each moment to the Eucharist so that each moment of our lives becomes a form of communion with the love of God. True, he says the Holy Eucharist has a sacramental efficacy which the 'sacrament of the present moment' cannot have, but the grace of the moment can be experienced much more frequently. Thus we are nourished, strengthened, purified, enriched and sanctified by the fullness of the present moment.

In finding God in every moment, Jean-Pierre is applying what Ignatius taught him in the *Exercises* about finding God in all things.

The past and the future do not belong to the real; only the present is real. The Spirit is entirely 'now', and by living in the 'now' we are in touch with reality. This is the truth that Gerry Jampolsky makes the central point of his books, *Love is Letting Go of Fear, Goodbye to Guilt, Teach Only Love*. By living in the present moment, we avoid the guilt, remorse and hurts of the past, and the fears and anxieties that the future produces.

Often in prayer there is a force striving to push the experience away from the 'now' and to transform an experience of the heart into one of the mind, to cause us to retreat into the past or look ahead to the future. Either way means moving from the real to the unreal. By heeding the advice of Jean-Pierre de Caussade and living in and with the sacrament of the present moment, we are nourishing the contemplative gift.

> . . . The life of faith is nothing less than the continued pursuit of God through all that disguises, disfigures, destroys, and, so to speak, annihilates Him.[9]

I have met a number of people who are trying to live a deep interior life and who keep worrying about whether they are doing God's will. Sometimes they say they would be at peace if they knew his will. Others see the will of God as something heavy, big, threatening, like some dragon in their path. At times they seem to me to have separated God's will from a loving God.

Then there are others who feel trapped by discussions about freedom, pre-destination and God's foreknowledge, and are uneasy about the term 'the will of God'. Because of all this, I prefer speaking of searching for God and not of seeking out his will.

The teaching of Jean-Pierre de Caussade about receiving God as he comes in each moment I find consoling. At times, of course, one will be required to discern the direction to take in one's life, and then the decision-making process enshrined in the *Spiritual Exercises* is a good guide. But most of the time we are not called to do that, and viewing the present as a revelation, an unveiling of God coming to us, preserves peace. This 'abandonment' to God is an essentially active embrace of the God of the present moment, not a passive, dispirited resignation. It is that which effectively works to renew the image of Jesus Christ deep within our hearts.

Again I find a parallel with the attitudinal development proposed by Jampolsky. What Jean-Pierre advocates is a change of heart towards all the events of each day. If I am able to see them as disguises God wears as he comes to me, my attitude will be welcoming. That approach is advocated by Merlin Carruthers in his several books about praise. Praising God for whatever happens accepts that 'for those who love God all things work for good'.

The sacrament of the present moment enables us to see beyond our senses and our reason, says de Caussade, and to live according to faith. 'The present moment is like an ambassador who declares the will of God. The heart must ever answer, "Let it be so".'[10] 'I will confine myself solely to the duty of the present moment in order to prove my love and leave you free to do with me what you will.'[11]

The attitudes we develop always colour our perceptions, and so influence what we think and feel. Jean-Pierre de Caussade offers attitudes that lead to wholeness.

Prayer

Jean-Pierre is a wise and safe prayer guide. His letters, in particular, show how he has absorbed the teaching of Ignatius, Teresa and John of the Cross, and how gently, in the spirit of St Francis de Sales, yet firmly, he directs the sisters in prayer. Letter VIII, book II, written to Sister Marie-Anne-Thérèse de Rosen in 1731, is a fine example. He writes that the most perfect prayer is the simplest. In this prayer there is less preoccupation with self—our ideas, imaginations, reasonings. Instead there is just one single sentiment or theme that is long drawn out and continues to hold us.[12]

'Beginning with this prayer of simplicity, which in reality is the second method of prayer prescribed by his Master, St Ignatius Loyola,

Caussade easily leads by way of self-abandonment to the highest union with God.' So judges Archbishop Goodier in his Foreword to Thorold's translation of *Spiritual Letters of Père de Caussade.*[13] Jean-Pierre speaks of simply gazing, gently recalling the mind, and above all the heart, to God's presence. When distracted, one should note the feelings with which prayer is ended and see the value of dryness and aridity. The director should lead by love and confidence and be encouraging.

Following Teresa's example, he says: 'the heart reposing sweetly in God, loves him without distinguishing clearly the object of its love, or how this love is produced in it'.[14] He is very encouraging, like Francis de Sales, using phrases like 'gently, sweetly and peacefully'. Again he watches to safeguard the encounter against reflections on the self and one's way of praying. He is alert to the danger of turning the prayer into a self-conscious performance. His maxim is: flowing gently with the Holy Spirit is the way to deeper union with God.

The letters of Jean-Pierre de Caussade are filled with good counsel for growth in prayer. His two books provide the principles for living a richer spiritual life.

Reflections

1. Take, Lord
   and receive all my liberty,
   my memory, my understanding
   and my entire will,
   all that I have and possess.

   You have given all to me,
   to you, Lord, I return it.

   All is yours;
   do with it what you will.

   Give me only your love
   and your grace,
   that is enough for me.

   Read slowly the above prayer by St Ignatius, pausing where a word strikes you. Dwell there, relishing the word.

2. Play the tape 'Take, Lord', by the St Louis Jesuits (*Earthen Vessels*, N.A.L.R., Phoenix, Arizona). Express by dancing what this prayer means to you.

Dwell on the distinctions between toleration, resignation, stoical conformity, fatalistic acceptance, Ignatian indifference, despairing abandonment, and the self-abandonment of Jean-Pierre de Caussade. Do you prefer the traditional title *Abandonment to Divine Providence*, or *The Joy of Full Surrender*?

Recall an experience when you were able to surrender fully. Was it joyful? What did you need to be freed from? Talk it over with a friend.

3. Reflect upon and discuss what is meant by 'the sacrament of the present moment'. How do you react to the phrase? Consider how you may let it influence your life on this day. Before you go to sleep tonight, reflect back on what happened.

4. Compare the writings of Gerry Jampolsky, Merlin Carruthers and Jean-Pierre de Caussade. Do you think they help you in your prayer? What attitude frustrates you? Are you hopeful of doing anything about it? Can anything be done if you are not hopeful?

5. Jean-Pierre cites Mary's life as an example of surrendering to the will of God. Ask Mary to talk over with you some of her experiences. Questions might help the dialogue flow: 'What did it cost you, Mary? Was it difficult to say "Yes"? Did you ever have misgivings? Where did you get your support?'

Notes

1. Jean-Pierre de Caussade, *The Joy of Full Surrender*, translated by Hal M. Helms, Paraclete Living Library, 1985, p. 27.
2. ibid., p. 77.
3. ibid., p. 83.
4. Jean-Pierre de Caussade, *Spiritual Letters*, 2 volumes, translated by Algar Thorold, Burns Oates & Washbourne Ltd, London, 1948 vol. II, p. 76.
5. ibid., p. 77.
6. Dom John Chapman, *Spiritual Letters*, Sheed & Ward, New Ark Library, London, 1959, p. 24.
7. ibid., p. 29.
8. ibid., pp. 41, 42.
9. *The Joy of Full Surrender*, p. 38.
10. ibid., p. 61.

11. ibid., p. 74.
12. *Spiritual Letters,* p. 41.
13. ibid., Foreword. p. xi.
14. ibid., p. 44.

Reading List

Jean-Pierre de Caussaude, *The Joy of Full Surrender,* translated by Hal M. Helms, Paraclete Living Library, 1985.

The Spiritual Letters of Father J.P. de Caussade SJ, translated by Algar Thorold, Burns Oates & Washbourne Ltd., London, 1948.

Spiritual Letters of Jean-Pierre de Caussade, translated by Kitty Muggeridge, Collins Fount Paperbacks, London, 1986.

The Sacrament of the Present Moment, translated by Kitty Muggeridge, Collins Fount Paperbacks, London, 1981.

21.

Mary MacKillop

Mother Mary of the Cross

'You will have in you the strength, based on his own glorious power, never to give in, but to bear anything joyfully, thanking the Father who has made it possible for you to join the saints and with them to inherit the light.'—(Colossians 1: 11,12)

'If you can have some share in the sufferings of Christ, be glad, because you will enjoy a much greater gladness when his glory is revealed. It is a blessing for you when they insult you for bearing the name of Christ, because it means you have the Spirit of glory, the Spirit of God resting on you.'—(1 Peter 4: 13-15)

These words of St Paul and St Peter are verified in the remarkable life of Australia's well known Mary MacKillop. She was born on 15 January 1842, in Brunswick Street, Fitzroy, Victoria, the eldest of a family of eight. Her parents were both from Scotland, and they had met and married in Australia. Mary paid tribute to her family for their love and care. Yet she also said that her childhood was unhappy partly because of the responsibility thrust upon her. Life on a farm, shop assistant with Sands-Kenny (later Sands & McDougall), governess, teacher at

Portland, Victoria and then at Penola, South Australia—such was her early life. Her meeting as a young woman with Father Julian Edmund Tenison Woods proved important, for she could talk to him about her desires for the religious life.

In 1866 she took charge of the Penola school, and during that year made a final decision to embrace religious life. The following year Father Tenison Woods drew up the first Rule of the Order of the Sisters of St Joseph of the Sacred Heart. Sister Mary and Sister Rose Cunningham opened the order's first school in Adelaide on 2 July 1867, and Mary took vows on 15 August that same year.

Early rapid expansion was followed by troubles and on 22 September 1871, Mary was excommunicated by Bishop Sheil for alleged disobedience. It was a sorry story compounded by the bishop's sickness, forces opposed to Father Tenison Woods and Mother Mary, the financial problems of the diocese and misunderstandings. The ban was lifted on 23 February 1872, just before Bishop Sheil died.

Acting on advice, on 28 March 1873, Mary went to Rome to seek approval of the Rule. She returned to Adelaide on 4 January 1875 with approval for the Constitutions, as well as fifteen Irish postulants. At the first General Chapter, she was elected Superior General.

The order's expansion continued, but so also did the opposition of some of the Irish bishops to the Constitutions. They wanted diocesan control, while Mary believed that central authority was essential to safeguard the original spirit of the order. In 1883 a Commission of Enquiry was set up by Bishop Reynolds and he deposed Mary and ordered her to leave Adelaide.

The Bishop of Bathurst and the Bishop of Brisbane had both opposed central government. When the Bishops' Synod in Sydney voted fourteen to three against central government, Mary's cause seemed lost. But she had good friends in Rome and also in Cardinal Moran, and on 25 July 1888 a decree from Rome constituted the Sisters of St Joseph of the Sacred Heart as an approved Regular Congregation with Mother House in Sydney. For twenty-one years Mary had battled for the vision that she and Father Tenison Woods had shared in Penola and Adelaide.

Now began the work of consolidation. Mary was elected General in 1899, and again in 1905, despite the stroke she suffered in 1902. She died on 8 August 1909.

Such is a brief outline of the events in her life. It is, however, her spiritual life that most concerns us here. Fortunately her letters, circulars, and diaries help us to see something of her union with God. Like Thérèse of Lisieux (1873–1897) she seems to have been drawn to enter deeply into the paschal mystery and to have been gifted in an extraordinary way. So I do not hesitate in placing her among those who were called into a true mystical encounter with God.

Prayer Life

When Mother Mary went to Rome seeking papal approval of the Constitutions, she wrote a letter to Monsignor Kirby, Rector of the Irish College, Rome, dated Ascension Thursday 1873. In it she wrote that she felt 'strongly urged to lay open to you the whole state of my mind, in so far as I can explain it, showing the wonderful care with which our dear Lord has watched over me.'[1] It is a very open account of her 'journey with God', beginning with her early childhood. 'My life as a child was one of sorrows, my home when I had it, a most unhappy one.' Yet she pays a loving tribute to both her father and mother. This fair-minded judgment of events and people characterises her whole life, being able to see the good as well as the less than good in a balanced way. The desire to be a religious was there, but the way was not clear because of her family responsibilities.

Her one guiding principle was God's will. 'Oh, Father, I cannot tell you what a beautiful thing the will of God seems to me.' 'To me, the will of God is a dear book which I am never tired of reading, which has always some new charm for me.' Towards the end of her life she stressed the same fidelity to the will of God.

She writes this about her prayer:

> I meant to tell you how I prayed, and to ask you to help me, but you may see from this our dear Lord does all, I do nothing. His presence is before me almost in everything, and I love to come to Him in prayer as to my dearest and only Friend. I do not care for using books at prayers—unless it be at meditation or other prayers in Community. At other times these would seem obstacles, something stepping in between the freedom and ease with which, like a child to a fond parent who she knows is ready to listen to her, I love to go to Him. But for all that, I serve Him with so little love, so little perfection, or attempt at them, in my ordinary actions.

She was then thirty-one years old and had been a religious for six years. She had been tried in the fire of much suffering caused by ill health, a lack of support from Father Tenison Woods, and condemnation by her own bishop. This account of her prayer shows her growing freedom and desire to be with her God.

There is another precious document that reveals how prayer for her was an encounter with her loving God, not a performance coming out of guilt. This is dated 28 March 1874, a year after the previous letter, while she was still in Rome. It is her confession for her Retreat and reads in part:

> As clearly, and often perhaps as forcibly as if He [Jesus] were visible to my bodily eyes, I have felt *Him* pleading in my heart, or encouraging me, or urging me on to some little act for His love. Sometimes it is sweet union with Him under a trial or disappointment, sometimes embracing willingly, or going forth to meet humiliations, sometimes deigning to stay with me in the strangest scenes (and never more intimately than then) . . . Sometimes, and oh with how much reason, reproaching me with considering creatures so much and *Him* so little, with many omissions of duty for this reason, etc. In the face of so much love, grace and mercy, I feel myself far more guilty in His pure sight than the greatest public sinner who ever lived.
>
> As His Spouse I feel that I should be equally interested in all that is dear to His Heart. For this reason He often seems to show me that He wants a purely disinterested and generous love, a love which does not tie me to some thing more than another in His service. To explain, whilst I feel that in the particular charge to which he has called [me], He looks for great fidelity and zeal, I at the same time feel as it were an intense craving on His part that I should serve Him with a big heart, not one only large enough for these particular duties, but one large enough to help Him and struggle for His interests in every earthly way that He puts before me. Dear Father, you have never spoken to me more plainly nor any other earthly friend, than I have often felt, or do feel, our dearest Lord speaking, craving in this way, in my heart.

The partial record of a later retreat made in October 1877 shows the influence of the *Spiritual Exercises* of St Ignatius Loyola. Her early steps towards and in religious life had been guided by Father Julian Tenison Woods, and for this she was ever grateful. Gradually, though, she began to lose confidence in his style of spirituality and was concerned about his too ready acceptance of the 'visionary sisters', and supposed revelations. Nor was she alone in this. So she began to rely on the Jesuits at Norwood, Fathers Hinteroecker and Tappeiner.

No doubt through them she was introduced to the *Spiritual Exercises* Her notes from the retreat of October 1877 show her faithfully following the programme. She cannot reason much; there is no need to because her will acts easily. Despite 'the strange dryness', hers is prayer from the heart. Clearly she is aware of the movements taking place in her soul, and the central theme of her spirituality, 'the will of God', is very evident. Feeling sick she has the freedom to curtail the prayer and go to bed. Her obedience to her director is evident. This spirituality is far removed from the path that Father Woods was taking, and shows how these two gifted souls were diverging in their experiences.

We have fuller notes for the retreat Mary made at Kensington in South Australia, from 10 to 19 March 1882, just prior to the terrible storm of the episcopal visitation. There is the same prayer: humbly placing herself in the presence of God. Often prayer becomes simpler and also Trinitarian, and this seems to be the path Mary's prayer is taking. Three days of the retreat are given to the first week of the *Spiritual Exercises*, and her notes speak of how she must give more loving service:

> I have been brought into his immediate service and have opportunities given to me to advance in the perfection of my state. But how, my God, have I used these opportunities! Too sadly forgetful of all—I have abused thy gifts by my impatience under trial, not seeing Thy Will in things painful to me. Forgive me, my God, and help me by Thy Grace to amend. Mary my Mother and St Joseph, pray for me.

She spent two days on the second week *Exercises*. The Reign of Christ, the Incarnation and the Nativity fill out the first of these days.

'I must love crosses and trials to please him and try to keep as near Him as possible . . . I must watch over the spirit of obedience in myself . . . taking in all things the example of my Jesus flying into Egypt as my guide.' When deposed and exiled so unjustly by Bishop Reynolds, did Mary, I wonder, recall this retreat resolution? Certainly she kept it.

And on to the Hidden Life, Jesus in the Temple, the Two Standards, the Three Classes:

> Under Thy standard alone shall I live and die . . . with all my heart I entreat Thee to do with me what thou pleasest. Crosses, contradictions and humiliations may be felt by my weak nature, but my heart and soul will welcome them as bringing me nearer to Thy love. I fear I shall fail sometimes—but my will is Thine. O my God, grant me grace to be faithful.

Certainly Mary MacKillop's spirituality is very much in touch with the reality of her own life. Soon she was to face the episcopal visitation made by Bishop Reynolds, which resulted in her exile from South Australia. This was worse than the excommunication, but the God of her prayer supported her.

On the sixth day of her retreat she moved on to the third week of the *Exercises.* So she writes: 'My loving Jesus, O grant me grace to be true to the great desire I now feel to suffer with and for Thee in whatever way Thou pleasest'.

Next day she is still praying about the Passion and writes:

> O let not thy Precious Blood be shed in vain. By the sacred fruits of it I entreat thee to nail my heart henceforth to Thy Cross and never let it stray again from Thee. O Mother of Sorrows, take with me St John as Thy child and plead for me when I am in danger of being unfaithful. St Joseph, pray for me.

On the final day of her retreat, she prays over the Resurrection scenes and the love of God. What is very striking about this prayer is the purification she has experienced through the dark nights of the senses and spirit, to use John of the Cross' words. Her summary reads:

> My glorified Jesus, my heart desires to rejoice with Thee today and to love and praise Thee for ever. Would that I could imitate now and always the dispositions of holy Magdalene. Would that I could love Thee as she did . . . But I am not worthy to feel this great love though I desire it with all my heart. I am content never to feel it here below, more than content, my God, as long as I can please Thee in all things and never again give Thee pain.
>
> *Here* let me work and suffer now as it pleases Thee. I ask and know that I deserve no sensible comfort on this earth. It is even too much comfort to know that I may serve Thee here below without any other joy than the thought that Thou art pleased to will it and to accept my imperfect service. Work and suffering *here* in union with Thee and Thy Will—and this for as long or as short as Thou pleasest—and *rest* and joy in Thy love when it may please Thee to call me to both in Heaven.

At this stage of her life Mary was forty years of age, and had been a religious for fifteen years. Her struggle for central government was continuing and she was about to suffer her trial, the episcopal visitation. Ill health continued to plague her. She made eight resolutions at the end of the retreat and on 23 April she reviewed them to see how she had fared. It is all very down to earth and Ignatian, this review. She writes:

> Five weeks today since the last day of my happy retreat—and as yet very little improvement in me, my God . . . I wish I could have more regular duties and then it would be easier to keep my resolutions. But would this be *Thy Will,* my God? Is it for my own pleasure even in Thy service that I desire to live? Ah no—only I am so weak. But keep

me in heart and will always near Thee and Thy Cross.

I do not ask Thee to give me good health—but, O my God, I entreat Thee not to let those sicknesses to which I am so subject interfere with my duty to Thee and my charges.

In the days following she wrote reflections on *The Imitation of Christ*, which she had been reading. She was puzzled at the contradiction she noted in herself: the little crosses seemed harder to bear than the big ones.

Entering the Paschal Mystery: Mary and St John of the Cross

All through Mary's life there are signs of a call to enter into the paschal mystery. On 23 November 1869—two years after she took her vows—Mother Mary wrote to Father Woods:

> Tomorrow is the Feast of St John of the Cross. I had intended in my letter last night to have asked you to pray for me in tomorrow's Mass. I never told you the almost clinging kind of devotion I feel towards that saint—I think that he and St Gertrude were the two I had naturally most devotion to, and how I first heard of him I cannot remember. It was before I came to Adelaide, and I do not yet know what there is in him that I feel so much attraction for. Surely it must be God has given me this longing for his patronage and that of St Gertrude, and if so, he will pray for me tomorrow. Will you entreat this favour for me?

Both these saints are mystics who suffered greatly. Gertrude was a German nun who lived in the thirteenth century and whose union with the person of Christ was, like Teresa's and John of the Cross' nuptial mysticism. Often she was too ill to be present at all the Choral Offices. John of the Cross, as we have seen, suffered much opposition, even imprisonment, in his work with Teresa for reform. The attraction Mother Mary of the Cross had for John of the Cross and Gertrude was surely given by God, as she says. The Cross dominated Mary's life and her devotions.

She herself wrote in a circular on May 21, 1877:

> In general, her month [May was dedicated to the Mother of God] has been one of crosses and trials to us—and this year it has been rich in them. Instead of being discouraged at this, we should rather rejoice and thank God for giving us such solid proofs of His love. But, dear Sisters, do we take crosses and trials as proofs of God's Love?

The story of Mary's excommunication is a sad one for all concerned. In a letter to Father Woods she writes:

> When the next morning I was called into the presence of the Bishop, I felt whilst in the Community room confused, lonely and bewildered. It was an intense relief when the Bishop ordered me to kneel down . . . I think I seemed not to realize the presence of the Bishop and priests. I know I did not see them, but I felt oh, such love for their office, a love and sort of reverence for the very sentence which I then knew was being in full force passed upon me. I do not know how to describe the feeling but that I was intensely happy and felt nearer to God than I had ever felt before. I can only dimly remember the things that were said to me, but the sensation of the calm beautiful presence of God I shall never forget . . . I loved the Bishop and priests, the Church and my good God more than ever. I did not feel alone, but I cannot describe the calm beautiful something that was near.

In the letter she wrote to her mother three weeks later there is no bitterness, just a concern for the 'poor Bishop' and a desire to understand, not condemn him.

An account to Father Woods of her feelings the night of the excommunication reads:

> Though obliged to go to bed, it was about 3 o'clock before I could sleep. I thought of the awful nature of the sentence and all that I had ever felt when hearing of such things before came to my mind. I thought of the state in which I was, supposing I should die before morning, but with this thought came a calm resigning of myself into the arms of my good God when I was then most lovingly reminded that I was far from feeling rebellious towards my Bishop . . . In the end I went to sleep very happily with more *loving* confidence in my good God than I had felt for a long time.

In an earlier letter of 26 September, she had written to encourage Father Woods and on 11 October she had written to tell him, 'I have never enjoyed so sure and certain peace of mind as of late.' She expressed gratitude for the support of Father Tappeiner and the other Jesuit Fathers.

On 6 November she wrote:

> I am a wanderer having no settled place to stay in, and obliged to avoid as much as possible your brother's house. But yet I am generally happy and have been made to promise *not to run away*. Have courage, dear Father, and pray for me.

On 15 November 1871 she wrote to Father Woods: '...I have only been able to ask dear St Gertrude to help and protect you. I think she has helped me ... I feel very happy today, dear Father, though full of some cares'.

When she wrote to her mother after the Bishop lifted his sentence, she accepted that 'God has wisely permitted it for a hidden and mysterious end. I hope that our common sorrow has done us all good'. She was quick to add: 'But *my* path, my dearest Mamma, will yet be that of the cross. I seek nothing else—and oh, I love and bless the sweet will which gives this chosen portion to me.' She wrote of the strength gained through the events, and again, 'The Cross is my portion—it is also my sweet rest and support. I could not be happy without my cross—I could not lay it down for all the world would give. With the Cross I am happy, but without it would be lost.'

Mary was uncompromising in adhering to the two foundations of the Institute—central government and poverty. She was convinced that the Institute was not 'a merely human invention', as she wrote to Bishop Sheil. The new Bishop Reynolds supported her at first, but then in 1883 began the Commission of Enquiry, which Sister Monica said was worse than the excommunication. Mary had many anxieties leading up to this and had seriously intended sending her resignation to Rome. In August 1883 she wrote: 'Between one thing and another I am nearly crushed. It would not matter if I were well, but I am not.'

On 13 November Bishop Reynolds wrote an extraordinary letter of censure, which deposed her and exiled her to Sydney. That letter would continue to give her nightmares in later years. Yet she replied: 'The instructions in your last letter surprised me but I submit'. In the interests of charity and peace, to avoid scandal, she went, careful to preserve the good name of the Bishop. We can see what it cost her from what she wrote to Sister Mechtilde in December:

> I am sorry for him, but night and day cannot forget his cruel writings to me ...It was a mercy that I was sent away else I should have gone mad, I think ...I am wonderfully free from any anxiety as to the future for out of the bitter cross unity and love will come.'

In his action Bishop Reynolds overstepped his powers, just as Bishop Sheil had. Yet we never find bitterness or self-pity in Mary, even though at times she was discouraged. By 'leaning on God' she continued her struggle for her beloved Institute. On her profession day Mary had accepted from Father Woods her new name 'Mary of the Cross' and throughout her life she responded courageously and humbly to her call to walk with Jesus in the paschal mystery.

The Institute that she and Father Woods started was revolutionary in its concept of nuns living in small groups scattered throughout the wide land of Australia. This was a new vision for nuns and, as usually happens, the new provoked opposition born of fear. Her insistence on central government brought her into conflict with many Irish bishops whose vision was restricted to their own dioceses and states. Mary was ahead of her times with her Australian dream. Her commitment to the education of the poor was not always welcomed by bishops and priests hopelessly worried about finance. By keeping true to her conviction that the Institute was no human creation but God's work, Mary lived out her Way of the Cross. For much of her life she was a sign of contradiction.

I believe she is worthy to be classed with these others whose prayer was a living encounter with the God of love. To her, Christ crucified was no stranger. Like Jesus, who accepted the mission of Messiah that led to Calvary, Mary accepted God's will, despite heavy opposition, and walked with Jesus in the paschal mystery.

Reflections

1. 'To me, the will of God is a dear book which I am never tired of reading, which has always some new charm for me,' wrote Mother Mary MacKillop. Reflect upon her journey. Compare her writings with Jean-Pierre de Caussade's *Sacrament of the Present Moment.* Some find the will of God anything but 'a dear book'. What is your experience? Can you think of an occasion where it brought you 'some new charm'?

2. In her diary during a retreat in 1896 Mary wrote:

   > Father Hendle had given instruction—gave a contemplation on the Passion and heard my confession afterwards. *Result.* To please God I will forget all the past and seek no redress. 'Tis but a poor return for all that God has suffered for me. To *Him* be all honour and glory. To me, shame and contempt. May He in His mercy and compassion keep me faithful.

   Do you think that Mary's reflection shows that she had some difficulty with past struggles? Are you aware of past hurts that continue to hold you? Follow the example of Mary and take them to the suffering Christ.

3. In 1907 Mother Mary wrote a circular to her sisters: 'An Appeal of the Sacred Heart to a Weary, Disappointed Soul'. This is a deep sharing of her intimacy with the Sacred Heart. She writes:

> When storms rage, when persecutions or dangers threaten, I quietly creep into Its deep abyss; and securely sheltered there, my soul is in peace, though my body is tossed upon the stormy waves of a cold and selfish world.

This is a beautiful account of her experiences of the paschal mystery. Reflect on her excommunication and the Commission of Enquiry. In what way may the Sacred Heart be calling you to experience the paschal mystery? How do you feel about the call? What helped Mary to respond generously? How may you be helped?

4. Seven months before her death, Mary wrote: 'Today I have been much better than usual, and I have been all the morning waiting, but very few came. Even in my chair I can give you my blessing, which I do with all my heart, and ask your prayers.'

   Here we can see something of the loneliness of a once very active woman, longing for company. How do you feel as you think of lonely, sick people? In what way can they help you? How can you help them? Is loneliness a feature of your life? Was it a feature of Mother Mary's? Was it part of the life of Jesus?

5. When we read her retreat notes, letters, and circulars, what is so striking is the ordinariness of Mary MacKillop. There is little evidence of the extraordinary. The lines of Hopkins, 'Sheer plod makes plough down sillion shine', express her fidelity to the call to educate poor children. In that lay her mysticism of everyday life and the paschal mystery. Jesus was tempted to be extraordinary and not ordinary. How do I see my ordinariness? Do I worry too much about being so 'ordinary'? Do I see mystics as being extraordinary people, whereas I am just an ordinary person? Could it be that my perception of myself as being ordinary is hindering my mystical journey? Am I missing out on the sacrament of the present moment because I seek signs and wonders?

Notes

1. This and all the quoted material in this chapter is taken from the Archives of the Sisters of St Joseph, St Joseph's Generalate, North Sydney.

Reading List

The Resource Material issued by The Archives of The Sisters of St Joseph, St Joseph's Generalate, North Sydney.

These issues are fascinating first-hand material.

Marie Therese Foale RSJ, *The Josephite Story*, St Joseph's Generalate, Sydney, 1989.

William Modystack, *Mary MacKillop*, Rigby, Adelaide, 1982.

George O'Neill, SJ, *Life of Mother Mary of the Cross*, Pellegrini and Co., Sydney, 1931.

Osmund Thorpe CP, *Mary MacKillop*, Burns & Oates, London, 1957.

22.

Thomas Merton

Searching for God

Thomas Merton was born in 1915 in France and died in 1968 aged fifty-three. His father was a New Zealander, his mother American, and both were artists studying in France when they met and married. Thomas' brother, John Paul, was born in 1918. In 1921, their mother died of cancer. Their early schooling took place in the USA, then France, then England at Oakham. In 1931 their father died, and Thomas' godfather, Dr Tom Bennett, became his guardian. In 1933 he went to Cambridge University, but his time there was a disaster.

Thomas moved back to the USA to live with his grandparents, and in 1935 attended Columbia University, where he made firm friendships and graduated. In 1938 he became a Catholic and was drawn to apply to enter the Franciscans, but was not accepted. Next he joined the staff at St Bonaventure's, teaching English, and in December 1941, when nearly twenty-seven he joined the Cistercians (Trappists) at Gethsemani. He took Simple Vows in 1944, Solemn Vows in 1947, and was ordained to the priesthood in 1949, a few months after the publication of his autobiography, *Seven Storey Mountain*. In 1951 he was appointed Master of Scholastics, in 1955, Master of Novices, which position he held for ten years. When he was released from that important but heavy responsibility, he retired to live as a hermit in a cottage on the property. In 1968 he was granted permission to attend a conference at Bangkok.

On 10 December 1968, while on this Asian trip, Thomas Merton died accidentally from electrocution.

The fifty-three years of Merton's life were marked by upheavals and change. World War I changed Europe and America. The Great Depression was followed by World War II, the Korean War and the Vietnam War. Communism's control in Russia and China, Nazism and Fascism were all shaping the society he lived in. Rapid technological development made the world of the 1960s very different from the world he was born into in 1915.

The Church, too, experienced the winds of change as Vatican II wrestled with changing problems and searched for today's answers. Merton was very much a part of this world, even though he withdrew from it into a monastery when he was almost twenty-seven. He never forgot it and at different times during his twenty-seven years as a monk, he was deeply aware of it, and affected by its upheavals.

Seven Storey Mountain, written in 1944 and published in 1948, was a best-seller and launched Merton from the obscurity of Gethsemani into world publicity. By the date of his ordination, 26 May 1949, more than 400,000 copies had been sold. I read *Elected Silence*, the version edited and abridged by Evelyn Waugh for the English market, in the early 1950s, and still recall the powerful impact it made on me. At the time I was drawn by Merton's discovery of God's mercy and love for a self-destructing world, and his vision of love. Several extracts on these themes I wrote in my journal and I still have them.

The story of a twentieth century man caught up in a vision of his sinfulness, and being freed by the mercy of God reaching down to draw him into his love, gave hope and purpose in life to many who were shattered and disillusioned by two world wars, a depression, a peace that was no peace. Here was Merton's journey to God and with God, like another Augustine's *Confessions*, casting light in the darkness.

His journey begins, surely, with his naked prayer:

> My Lord God, I have no idea
> where I am going. I do not see the road
> ahead of me. I cannot know for certain
> where it will end. Nor do I really know
> myself, and the fact that I think I am

> following your will does not mean that
> I am actually doing so. But I believe
> that the desire to please does in fact
> please you. And I hope I have that desire
> in all that I am doing. I hope that I
> will never do anything apart from that
> desire. And I know that if I do this you
> will lead me by the right road, though I
> may know nothing about it. Therefore
> I will trust you always though I may
> seem to be lost and in the shadow of
> death. I will not fear, for you are ever
> with me, and you will never leave me to
> face my perils alone.

Thomas Merton did not have strong family support, or stability in his early years. At Cambridge he was a failure. In Rome, however, when he was eighteen he discovered something of Christ, followed by a vivid vision of his father. It did not last long, but it gave him a profound insight into his sinfulness, and for the first time he began to pray.[1] As far as I can judge, this was the beginning of a true conversion experience. Perhaps, too, the vision was an indication of what he later calls his bloody mysticism, his dark path. The experience bears the marks of a movement from the Good Spirit, since Merton is led to God, not to self-rejection.

The move to Columbia brought him people and books, both important for his journey. Daniel Walsh, Edward Rice, Bob Lax, Seymour Freedgood, Mark Van Doren, gave him the acceptance needed to heal the pain of his rejections. Huxley, Gilson, Blake, Maritain and Hopkins gave him a balanced diet for mind and heart. Throw in Joyce, *The Imitation of Christ, The Confessions of St Augustine, The Spiritual Exercises of St Ignatius Loyola,* and something had to happen. In *Seven Storey Mountain* he tells us that he was reading Father Lahey's life of Hopkins when there was movement in him 'that spoke like a voice'. 'What are you waiting for?' it said. 'Why are you sitting here? Why do you still hesitate? You know what you ought to do. Why don't you do it?' The part he was reading told of Hopkins writing to Newman about his indecision. For some time Merton struggled with this, then he went to see Father Ford. He was walking in the light rain towards Broadway, when 'everything inside me began to sing—to sing with peace, to sing with strength and to sing with conviction'. His decision to become a Catholic was confirmed by the spiritual consolation he enjoyed.

The idea of being a priest came to him, and stayed. He applied to join the Franciscans, but was refused. In April 1941 he made a retreat at Gethsemani, the Trappist Monastery. A few months later he helped out at Friendship House in Harlem and talked with Catherine von Hueck (Doherty). He was now torn between the Trappists and Friendship House. In December he decided to join the Trappists at Gethsemani, and on 21 February 1942 he was accepted as a choir monk, Brother M. Louis Merton OCSO.

Since he had vowed stability, one might think he had reached his haven, 'where no winds blow'. Yet the twenty-seven years he spent with the Trappists were filled with the same searching for God, and with struggles as exhausting and, I think, deeper than those of the twenty-seven years that brought him to Gethsemani. Censorship was a continual problem, as he reconciled himself to obedience. Later he said that obedience was much more difficult than poverty and chastity. A narrow interpretation of obedience was in conflict with the winds of change in the Church that were opening up doors to more mature responsibility for religious. Thomas Merton had come to the order to find solitude. Community life was not giving him that experience. He applied to join the Carthusians and thought of the Camaldolese, where he would be able to live alone, but his application was refused.

All this created great tension in him. His relationship with the abbot Dom James Fox seems to have been ambivalent. If he could not become a Carthusian, why not be a hermit, live apart, within the Trappists? He explored this possibility and during the 1960s he moved in this direction. At that time, he was also drawn into the great world issues of peace, war, racial justice, poverty and Ecumenism. He had a steady stream of visitors and undertook voluminous correspondence and the writing of articles and books. He felt the call to travel and to become involved, but his superiors were not convinced that his vocation lay there.

His health was poor and he suffered much pain, with many visits to the hospital. When he fell in love with a student nurse and she with him, he wondered about leaving the Monastery and marrying. Yet he was not convinced that he should leave Gethsemani, so he stayed.

His study of Zen, Buddhism and Sufism was drawing him more strongly towards the East. In the 1960s Ecumenism was not as respectable as it is today, nor was there the appreciation of Eastern Religions that one now finds. Merton was a pioneer in this field, and he suffered as all pioneers do.

From all this turmoil, the question arises: why did he stay? Rice says he was not happy. I think there is much evidence against this. Although his path was dark, there was also light. He was not the only pilgrim to be caught in the confusion of his times, and yet to grow through it all.

On Prayer

Thomas Merton is a valuable guide for those seeking help in prayer, although there is not a great deal written about his own way of praying. In fact, he was quite reserved about it. In a letter, however, to the Sufi scholar Aziz Ch. Abdul, he details his daily programme in his hermitage, during the last years of his life. In addition to study, Mass and Office, he had three sessions of meditation daily, each lasting an hour or so. His meditation was simple, centred entirely on the presence of God and his will and his love. 'It is centred on faith, by which alone we can know the presence of God.' He used no images of God and no thinking about God. This letter clearly shows that he is following the apophatic or non-conceptual tradition of prayer.

Merton went to bed at 7.30 p.m. and rose about 2.30 a.m.[2] He wrote:

> I am still a 14th century man: the century of Eckhart, Ruysbroeck, Tauler, the English recluses, the author of *The Cloud,* Langland and Chaucer—more an independent and a hermit than a community man, by no means an ascetic, interested in psychology, a lover of the dark Cloud in which God is found in love. This is what I am: I must consent to it and not be ashamed that I am not something more fashionable.[3]

For years he had been led by John of the Cross. In 1961 he talked of his discovery of Julian of Norwich and Meister Eckhart. 'Julian is without doubt one of the most wonderful of all Christian voices. She gets greater and greater in my eyes as I grow older.'[4]

Another powerful influence on his spiritual life was the spirituality of the East. Huxley's *End and Means,* the friendship with the Hindu monk Bramachari during student days (ironically the Hindu told him to read *The Imitation of Christ* and St Augustine's *Confessions*) planted the seed that flowered in his later attraction to Sufism, Buddhism, Zen, and Hinduism, and climaxed in his Asian journey.

His *Spiritual Journals* record his inner life. Publication of these was forbidden until twenty-five years after his death. But though we do not yet know much about his personal prayer, he wrote much about prayer in general and he gave instructions. With its down-to-earth-simplicity, rugged honesty, and encouragement, his teaching has helped many.

Contemplative Prayer, one of the last books he wrote, is 'a practical non-academic study of prayer', written expressly for monks, but, as Merton says, of interest to all Christians. I found it excellent.

Harvey Egan notes that Merton's writings have a Teresian flavour to their style, but show the influence of John of the Cross in the apophatic themes he keeps returning to: the divine darkness, the radical emptiness and the desert experience.[5] Merton differs from the two great Carmelite doctors in the way he blends in the East and the social struggles of his time. In style he is conversational, as is the author of *The Cloud,* but in *The Cloud* there is no mention made of fourteenth-century upheavals. Merton further differs from Teresa and John and *The Cloud* in his profound emphasis on the significance of mysticism not only for individual transformation, but also for social change.

In *Contemplative Prayer* Merton writes well of the prayer of the heart, and of obstacles to meditation. One obstacle is making ourselves the subject of the meditation, as we reflect on our progress, our faults, our security and so on. I regard this as a second sign that we are meeting the God of the Hundred Per Cent. (The first sign is the belief that this false God loves us conditionally.) Herein lies the danger I sometimes see in so much self-searching through psychological testing.

Prayer is an encounter with God, not self. Merton tells us to 'seek God himself present in the depths of our being and meet him there by invoking the name of Jesus in faith, wonder and love'. So we seek the deepest ground of our identity in God. Prayer just means yearning for the simple presence of God. It is thus that I discover who I am. I am myself a word spoken by God. A word spoken by God must have meaning. The true self is hidden in obscurity and 'nothingness', at the centre, where we are directly dependent on God.

Merton is helpful in his writing about John of the Cross and the Dark Nights, and in his warnings against quietism.

Some fundamental principles of prayer as taught by Merton are:

1. Begin with reality—where you are. God is within you. In the prayer of the heart we seek first of all the deepest ground of our identity in God. Prayer means yearning for the simple presence

of God. It is the longing in my heart for my God—so personal, so intimate. See Psalms 42 and 63. Be aware, attentive, open to God and his personal love for you.

2. Avoid the impractical idealism of 'expecting the wrong thing: I keep control, I decide what is to happen, this way suits me', and so on.

   Avoid passive realism: 'This is the way it is, so what can you do about it?' This approach expects nothing.

   Both result from self-fulfilling prophecies and disregard of God's love. The remedy? Expectant faith.

3. Be open to the world, to its struggles, etc.

4. Remember that aridity—the dead spots in our prayer—is important.

Reflections

1. Re-read Merton's prayer on page 180, slowly and thoughtfully. Pause on any part that strikes you.

   Reflect on Merton's journey. Do you note any relevances in this prayer to his pilgrimage of faith?

   Reflect now on your own pilgrimage. Are there any parallels with the prayer, and/or with Merton's experience?

2. In a letter to Aziz Ch. Abdul, Thomas Merton wrote:

   > Now you ask about my method of meditation. Strictly speaking, I have a very simple way of prayer. It is centered entirely on attention to the presence of God and to His will and His love. That is to say that it is centered on *faith*, by which alone we can know the presence of God. One might say that this gives my meditation the character described by the Prophet as 'being before God as if you saw Him.' Yet it does not mean imagining anything or conceiving a precise image of God, for that to my mind would be a kind of idolatry . . . There is in my heart this great thirst to recognize totally the nothingness of all that is not God. My prayer is then a kind of praise rising up out of the centre of nothing and silence . . .

> Such is my ordinary way of prayer or meditation. It is not 'thinking about' anything, but a direct seeking of the Face of the Invisible—which cannot be found unless we become lost in Him who is invisible.[6]

Is your understanding of this prayer experiential or simply intellectual?

3. Thomas Merton continues to be a popular guide in prayer. Do you find help in him? If so, what is it that appeals? Discuss with a friend the ideas and feelings you have.

Notes

1. Edward Rice, *The Man in the Sycamore Tree*, Image Books, Doubleday, New York, 1972.
2. Michael Mott, *The Seven Mountains of Thomas Merton*, Sheldon Press, London, 1984, pp. 432, 433.
3. ibid., p. 362.
4. ibid., p. 362.
5. Harvey Egan SJ, *Christian Mysticism*, Pueblo Publishing Company, New York, 1984, p. 215.
6. Michael Mott, *The Seven Mountains of Thomas Merton*, p. 433.

Reading List

Thomas Merton, *The Seven Storey Mountain*, Harcourt Brace Jovanovich, San Diego, 1948.

Thomas Merton, *Seeds of Contemplation*, Anthony Clarke Books, Hertfordshire, paperback edition, 1972.

Monica Furlong, *Merton, A Biography*, Harper & Row, New York, 1985.

Michael Mott, *The Seven Mountains of Thomas Merton*, Sheldon Press, London, 1984.

William Shannon, *Thomas Merton's Dark Path*, Farrar, Straus and Giroux, New York, 1981.

Harvey Egan SJ, *Christian Mysticism*, Pueblo Publishing Company, New York, 1984.

23.

Gerhard Pieper SJ

An Ordinary Man

I introduce now an unknown mystic, one who was very ordinary and yet whose journey was ended by martyrdom. I include his story here because our paths united us with mutually enriching love, and because he illustrates for me the mysticism of everyday life and the paschal mystery. I welcome the opportunity of paying tribute to a dear friend.

Father Gerhard Pieper was born in Berlin on 18 June 1940. He entered the Society of Jesus in 1959 and was ordained to the priesthood in 1970. He taught chemistry at St Albert's Secondary School in northeast Rhodesia, but, as he wrote in September 1975, 'because of terrorist activities and other various reasons, we had to close our school this year, after the first term'. From November 1975 to August 1976, he was in Australia for his Tertianship, a spiritual renewal programme that Jesuits undertake a few years after their ordination. After his Tertianship he returned to Rhodesia.

He pronounced his Final Vows in 1977. By then he had already spent more than ten years in Rhodesia and was fluent in the Shona language, as well as being fluent in English and his native German. Sometime around 8.00 p.m. on 26 December 1978, he was shot to death by a youth among a band of young people who had come to his mission at Kangaire demanding food.

On the feast of St Stephen, the first martyr, Gerhard Pieper joined that heroic band of his brother Jesuits who had been killed in Rhodesia: Fathers Christopher Shepherd-Smith and Martin Thomas, and Brother John Conway, killed at Musami on 7 February 1977; Father Gregor Richert and Brother Bernhard Lisson, killed at Sinoia, on 27 and 28 June 1978; Father Desmond Donovan, who was abducted on 15 January 1978 and has not been heard of since. And he was reunited, too, with the other priests, brothers and sisters who had laid down their lives for Christ in Rhodesia—altogether, six priests, four brothers and six sisters—and two priests abducted and not heard of since.

My first meeting with Gerry, also called Peter, was in November 1975, when he came to join the Tertianship programme of which I was in charge. He was a cheerful extrovert and, as he told me later, he took to me immediately. So began a deep friendship between us. I was privileged to guide him through the *Spiritual Exercises* for thirty days and, during this time I saw the generosity of his commitment to the priesthood and his Jesuit vocation.

Gerry was very open and outspoken, and at times could be abrasive. But in his honesty he would talk about the problem and admit to the need for help in any area. On 18 January 1976, he wrote to me: 'The Jim Gill sessions produced a rather profound experience, an "everything-previous-falling-into place" experience. For me, everything else of the two months culminated there'. He was referring to the group encounter week that the Tertians had experienced under Father James Gill SJ, MD, as facilitator. The result of his Long Retreat and the Encounter was a very deep encounter with himself as he became more in touch with his own feelings.

In this letter to me he spoke of the child within him, often at odds with the adult. Thus he writes: 'In the following I shall try to let my "adult" speak to your "adult". You realise that this is a fairly novel experience for me, so please forgive the archaic "child" and "parent", when they break through'. Later he spoke about the growing together of the group, the intimacy that developed and his wish that ways could be found to promote further development. He commented:

> It could, however, be that in this wish my 'child' was hooked and wanted to leave problem solving and the effort at prayer in the care of others. In fact, the more I think of it, the more I think this to be true. If I had not grown I could have blamed it on others. (There is something helpful about feeling and thinking on paper!)

Later he made observations about the prayer sessions that were conducted by Father Tony de Mello SJ and referred to the fact that he

> rationalised my not-full participation with tiredness . . . My 'child' definitely had the upper hand—that is why I wanted you to kick me in the pants. I see now quite clearly that this would have been the worst thing you could have done to my growth. You treated me as an adult—a rare experience from a 'parent' figure. You did the unexpected and made me think. Thanks. The more I think about this incident, the more I love you and feel warm towards you . . .
>
> Again, sometimes I thought it would have been better for me if you had been overpowering. I realise now that my child wanted you to be the parent and that your love for me prevented you from becoming this.

He returned to the Jim Gill sessions and spoke positively of the gain to himself: 'I talked already about Jim. I copied his notes on me. It will be hard work, but he gave me hope. Hope for the future, I believe, has been one of the strongest feelings during these months.'

Summing up the fruits of these early months of the Tertianship, Gerry wrote:

> The emphasis on affectivity is healthy and not overdone. It was one of the factors which made me feel at home in spite of alien feelings concerning food and customs. Being embraced by you and others meant more than many words can say. Getting to know one's own people's feelings is often more important than to know what they think . . . On the whole, however, the atmosphere of love and trust in the group, which made the Jim Gill event possible for me, is the main impression . . . I gained a new knowledge of myself, a deeper love for Jesus, a new realisation of my vocation as a Jesuit. I received the great gift of being accepted by the group as I am.

After this phase of Tertianship Gerry worked in the North Sydney parish of St Marys and a few months later was part of the team of Tertians who gave directed retreats at Rosanna in Victoria. Of this he writes:

> Stage II was a great experience. The knowledge that we were to give retreats ourselves made our studies in Pymble very relevant. I told you already, Frank, what a valuable experience the actual retreat giving was for me. I felt very humble when I realised how the Spirit used me as his tool. I was amazed and full of gratitude when those four nuns responded to his guidance.

It came as no surprise that he made a Marriage Encounter Weekend and also involved himself in the Charismatic Renewal. He speaks of meeting Father 'Chuck' Gallagher SJ who was visiting Australia for Marriage Encounter.

Gerry's time in Australia proved a very rich experience, but he always knew that the call of Christ for him was to help spread the Kingdom in Rhodesia. He was too honest, however, with himself not to be aware of the pain leaving Australia would cost him. 'All in all I feel sad at the moment to have to leave here with the prospect of never seeing anybody again who was good to me.'

In August 1976 he returned to Rhodesia, but not to a school. His new assignment was Kangaire Mission, St Francis Xavier, Mount Darwin. There was tension there, and I recall a letter that told of the departure of the pastor because of the strain, and that Gerry was now on his own. He kept in touch by means of cyclostyled letters at the end of 1977 and also 1978. The one dated 8 December 1978 tells a story of persecution and inspiring faith. Since the outbreak of the war, six priests, four brothers and six sisters had been murdered by terrorists, and two priests had been abducted and were feared dead. Deported were nine priests, three sisters and one Jesuit scholastic. Arrested, tried or imprisoned were nine priests, one brother and seven sisters. Missions, schools and hospitals were closed. In many parts of Rhodesia, Christians were no longer allowed to meet for prayer.

Despite all this, Gerry could write:

> Our parish is still growing. Attendance at services increased by four persons per service. This might not sound very much, but is quite amazing under present conditions. While last year only thirty-five people attended our yearly retreat, this year there were over sixty. Also the attendance at baptism classes, singing courses, and parish council meetings has nearly doubled.

After describing the sufferings of the people from private armies and internment, Gerry says:

> Many of you might ask yourselves: Is there much point in all this? Should one just leave these people to their own devices? Why help, when surely everything will be destroyed again? Why invest money and hard work when these people are so ungrateful? Please, do believe me, if we went away now, we would be like the shepherd who deserts his sheep, because he is only a hireling. How could we ever again read the parable with a good conscience? Even the guerillas here in our area respect this attitude.

When I read this most moving appeal, I recall that Gerry once said to me: 'When you meet me, ask me two questions: "Are you growing in poverty of spirit?" and "Are you growing in your 'adult'?" '. His clear appraisal of the situation in Kangaire and his generous commitment to his people are clear indications that he had grown as he desired. The great call of the *Spiritual Exercises* to do 'more' for Christ, the offering of the meditation on the 'Two Standards', the deep poverty of spirit that is at the heart of the three degrees of humility—all of this had taken root in Gerry's heart. He knew that he had got much out of his Long Retreat and I remember his realistic comment that: '. . . it will take a lot of work to make this experience my own, to help my growth, and not stay just a beautiful dream'. The feast of St Stephen, 1978, is the proof that the dream had become the reality.

Here is a personal letter Gerry wrote to me:

> Dear Frank, Peace!
>
> Thank you for your long letter from Santa Barbara. If it were not for you, I should lose all contact with the S.J.'s in Australia. Have not heard from Kopek either for a long time. Marriage Encounter has arrived in Durban and is thriving. They got trained in Eire. Hopefully it should be here soon. I am glad you still enjoy being a Tertianmaster; I suppose after a while it becomes quite exhausting. Please, give my love to everybody I know. Lots of love,
>
> Gerry.

As I reflect on this letter, the last I received from Gerry, and as I reflect on his martyrdom on the feast of St Stephen, there comes to mind T.S. Eliot's 'Murder in the Cathedral' and the sermon preached by Thomas à Becket, Archbishop of Canterbury.[1] The text of the sermon is the message of the angels: 'Peace on earth', and that too was the opening of Gerry's 1978 Christmas letter: 'Christmas during wartime—the older ones of you might still have memories.' Gerry himself did; he was born during wartime, and the war had killed his father before he was born. Christmas during wartime—a contradiction? It is not easy to be happy and announce the Good News of the angels: 'Peace on Earth', when men nearby kill each other, when nearly every family in this country mourns a dear friend.'

But Gerry, like à Becket, does not lose heart: 'So there is still hope in spite of the difficult situation and the senseless slaughter of dear friends like Fr. Richert and Br. Lisson.' Where is this hope that Gerry saw? I think I find the answer in à Becket's sermon, an answer that is not an answer if we mean by that the solution to the problem. As à Becket said:

> A martyrdom is always the design of God, for his love of men, to bring them back to his ways. It is never the design of man; for the true martyr is he who has become the instrument of God, who has lost his will in the will of God, and who no longer desires anything for himself,

> not even the glory of being a martyr. Thus, as on earth the Church mourns and rejoices at one and the same time, in a fashion that the world cannot understand, so in Heaven the saints are most high, having made themselves most low, and are seen, not as we see them, but in the light of the Godhead from which they draw their being.

The murder of Gerry Pieper is not a senseless tragedy, but a mystery of love, and as such rests in the death of Jesus on Calvary. In his dying Gerry brings us face to face with mystery and invites us to stay with the mystery. When we live with mystery, we are touching the face of God.

To have known you, Gerry, to have walked with you along the path of the *Spiritual Exercises* for thirty days, to have shared in depth with you in the time we were together and to have known your hopes and fears—in all these Our Lord and Master is close to us. In your death, and the manner of it, the Crucified Lord is closer, or I should say—prompted by your German sense for accuracy!—makes us see how close he is.

Reflections

1. 'Train us, Lord, to throw ourselves into the impossible because behind the impossible is your grace and your presence: we cannot fall into a vacuum.'—Luis Espinal SJ, martyred in Bolivia, March 1980.

   Reflect on this prayer. What does it tell you about the gift of hope? Recall experiences in your own life when you seemed to hold on to hope against the odds.

2. 'You will have in you the strength, based on his own glorious power, never to give in, but to bear anything joyfully, thanking the Father who has made it possible for you to join the saints and with them to inherit the light.'—Colossians 1: 11,12

   Consider the above promise. Notice the keywords: 'strength', 'joyfully', 'thanking the Father'. Do you know any suffering people whose lives are a testimony to these words? Is any experience that you have had relevant? Think of Etty Hillesum, Joni Eareckson, Simone Weil, the film *My Left Foot,* Mary MacKillop, St Thomas More, St Maximilian Kolbe.

3. Simone Weil has said that suffering is too precious to be wasted. What is fruitful and creative about suffering? What are the perils? Draw upon your own experiences and talk this over with some friends.

4. The deeper that sorrow carves into your being,
   the more joy you can contain.
   Is not the cup that holds your wine the very cup
   that was burned in the potter's oven?
   And is not the lute that soothes your spirit,
   the very wood that was hollowed with knives?
   —Kahlil Gibran

   What is your immediate, spontaneous reaction to these words?

5. No clouds, no sunset.
   No Cross, no Crown.
   Whoever share my labours will share my glory.

   Try rephrasing these sayings to reflect situations in your own life.

Notes

1. T.S. Eliot, *Murder in the Cathedral,* Faber and Faber, London.

24.

The First Christian Mystic

Mystical Rose

The Mother of Jesus is the first Christian mystic, first in time and first in eminence. In her we find the richest embodiment of mysticism.

Union with God through a deep, transforming encounter with him and an ever-growing awareness of his intimate presence are at the heart of the mystical life. How true this is of Mary, his Mother.

No other human person was ever more united with Jesus Christ than Mary. There was the physical union of mother and child. 'I formed you in my womb,' she could have said as she read Psalm 139. He was flesh of her flesh, blood of her blood. But Jesus told us of an even deeper bond between them, as Luke records: 'As Jesus was speaking, a woman in the crowd raised her voice and said, "Happy the womb that bore you and the breasts that you sucked!" But he replied, "Still happier those who hear the word of God and keep it!"' (Luke 11: 27,28).

Far from in any way belittling their physical relationship, Jesus is directing us to their spiritual union. It is in Mary's willingness to hear God's word and to keep it that her true greatness lies. As St Augustine remarks, Mary conceived Jesus in her mind before she conceived him in her body.

Physically and spiritually she is at one with her man-God son. No other mystic experienced the union with which Mary was gifted. In her we see that union of likeness through love that John of the Cross describes.

Flowing from this deep union with Jesus came her knowledge of him. No human person knew Jesus as well as she did. She knew him as a mother loves her child. She had been with him on his life's journey, talking with him, seeing and pondering all the events of that life. The depth of her spiritual union with him helped her to enter more deeply into the mystery of his identity and enriched her own.

The growing intimate knowledge of God that we find in Julian of Norwich, Francis de Sales and others, and which comes from their mystical graces, is to be seen above all in Mary.

The Cloud of Unknowing described how God takes the initiative. The beginning of our prayer, the gentle stirrings towards God, are the Spirit's work in us. 'O gentle hand! O delicate touch!' cries out John of the Cross. 'The loving yearning of the soul through the touch of the Holy Spirit,' exclaims Julian. Their stories illustrate how God came into their lives with transforming love.

This too happens in the first recorded encounter of God with Mary. He begins the dialogue. Mary listens and is disturbed, afraid. God reassures, Mary listens. Prayer is a listening experience. Now she is puzzled, and speaks of this to God, who calls her from bewilderment to mystery, the mystery of his love for the human race. So she says 'yes' to a God who is turning her life upside down. Reading Luke's account of the Annunciation tells us much about prayer, and God's ways.

Mary's story reminds us of the entry of God into the lives of Ignatius, Francis of Assisi, Teresa of Jesus, Julian. In fact the Mother of Jesus played a part in their call. Julian treasured the vision she had 'of Our Lady St Mary . . . in her bodily likeness . . . of the stature she had when she conceived.' Jean-Pierre de Caussade finds in her *fiat*, her surrender to God's will, the model of faith.

It is the faith of Mary that inspires and leads to compassion. The inward journey is suspect if we are not led to reach out in love and compassion. Mary moves out to help her cousin Elizabeth and to share the rich experience of the Christ-coming. What God gives us is never for ourselves alone.

The visions of Julian lead her to compassion. Thomas Merton's search for God makes him compassionate toward the world he has left but which continues to involve him in its sufferings. My friend Gerry Pieper cannot leave his flock without a shepherd. All who encounter the God of compassion must cry and suffer with his children. A mysticism without compassion is no mysticism at all.

Calvary finds Mary close by the Cross of her Son. Sharing in the helplessness and pain of Jesus does not lead her into hopelessness, but rather into strong hope. This first mystic reveals that the gift of the paschal mystery is this strong hope. Mary MacKillop, struggling with smaller crosses, incredibly peaceful and strong during the big storms, gives us the same message. Ignatius, Francis, Etty, Joni, Corrie ten Boom, and all those whose lives are intimately linked with the paschal Lord, act as beacons to a world imprisoned by hopelessness.

Mary, 'the simple, humble maiden' seen by Julian, lived an ordinary life in Nazareth. The appeal of Mary MacKillop is a life that is so ordinary, without signs and wonders. Gerry Pieper was very ordinary. Teresa teaches that visions do not make her holy, *The Cloud* urges moderation. All these people and works are reminders that the essence of mysticism is union with God, not remarkable phenomena.

Julian, Ignatius and many others find that their prayer journey takes them to the Trinity. Of all mystics, Mary, the Mother of Jesus, is most caught up in the mystery of the Trinity. God the Father invites her to be the Mother of the Word made flesh, and she surrenders to the power of the Spirit. A Trinitarian mystic indeed, experiencing the joy of full surrender long before de Caussade wrote about it.

When the Spirit moves in her she utters the purest form of prayer, the prayer of praise (Luke 1: 26-38). The poetry of John of the Cross, the sensitive lyricism of Julian, the outpouring of the love in her heart by Etty, the prisoner of Westerbork, all join in the wonderful tribute of the Magnificat.

Some of our mystics—John of the Cross, Teresa of Jesus—describe what has been called bridal mysticism. The transforming, illuminating union of likeness is called spiritual espousals and spiritual marriage. How aptly this describes the union between the Trinity and Mary!

Others are said to be gifted with a mysticism of service. Francis de Sales, Mary MacKillop, Ignatius, Thomas Merton and de Caussade would qualify here. So also would Mary the Mother of God and the Mother of the Church. At Cana she was sensitively alive to the needs of others (John 2: 1-12). Paul VI's promulgation of her as Mother of the Church was stating what we all knew, for we had all experienced Mary's intercessory love. 'They have no wine' is her continuing prayer.

So often we see Mary guiding the first steps of a mystical journey. True to her title, Mother of the Sick, she appeared to Julian, Ignatius,

Francis de Sales and Thérèse of Lisieux, bringing healing. Mystics, no matter where we place their mysticism, are all called to bring the vision of their faith, the courage of their hope, the warmth of their love to a world that is sick because it has lost its God. Mary experienced the pain of such a loss and searched in anguish for Jesus when He was twelve years of age. At times Francis, Thomas Merton, Ignatius and Mary MacKillop all searched for their God in hiding. John of the Cross tells of the dark nights of the senses and the spirit, which in some smaller way echo the heartbreaking cry from the Cross, 'My God, my God, why have you forsaken me?' The Mother of Jesus would have felt the pain in her own heart, and so too does the mystic.

Without exception, all true mystics know that the foundation of holiness is humility. Mary responds to the greatest request God can make of a creature, saying simply, 'Behold the handmaid of the Lord. Be it done unto me according to your word'. Grounded in humility, she leads all mystics to an encounter with the God who loves them gratuitously and unconditionally. In their abandonment to divine providence they make surprise discoveries about their God, about themselves.

So they invite us all to join them, to come from behind our walls, to discover that 'My beloved is mine and I am his'.

Reflections

1. Read through the Song of Songs 2:8 and 3:5 and Luke 1: 26–38. Compare the coming of the lover to the beloved with God coming to Mary at the Annunciation. In the Song the lover at first meets the walls the beloved is hiding behind. What do you think these walls are? How does the lover entice the beloved from behind her walls? What are the walls Mary is hiding behind? How does God draw her from behind these walls?

2. Reflect on an experience in your life when God came to you. Did he meet you immediately, or your walls? If you were hiding, what were the walls you hid behind, and how were you released? Do you still have walls that keep you from intimacy with God and people? Do you see yourself as God's 'beautiful one'?

3. Think of five joyful mysteries in your life and say the Rosary with *your* five joyful mysteries. Do you think that this way of praying can bring you to wholeness? If so, why?

4. Read through the Magnificat slowly. Now write your own Magnificat, your own prayer of praise for the way God is working in your life. Do you find this easy or difficult? Listen to what your feelings may be telling you about your attitude to God, to yourself.

5. What is your favourite scene in Mary's life? Ponder it deeply in your heart. How do you see it in relationship to yourself and God right now? What is attractive about this scene? Which scene in Mary's life presents difficulty to you? What is the difficulty and what causes it?

   In prayer, talk over with Mary your experiences with both scenes.

6. Read slowly the story of the loss and finding of Jesus in the temple (Luke 2: 41-52). What feelings do you think Mary had during the search? Construct the conversation between Mary and Joseph. What feelings do you think Mary had when they found Jesus? How do you react to the answer that Jesus gave his parents? Is there any similar experience of searching in either your life or your prayer? Any puzzling answer? Any unanswered questions? Imagine you are told by God that you can talk this over with either Jesus or Mary or Joseph. Whom would you choose? Why that choice? Write out the dialogue between the two of you.

Reading List

E. Schillebeeckx, *Mary, Mother of The Redemption,* Sheed & Ward, London, 1964.

Karl Rahner, *Mary, Mother of The Lord,* Herder Freiburg/Nelson, London, 1963.

J.P. Kenny SJ, *The Meaning of Mary for Modern Man,* Spectrum Publications, Melbourne, 1980.

'The Dogmatic Constitution of the Church' (Lumen Gentium), Chapter VIII: 'The Role of the Blessed Virgin Mary, Mother of God, in the Mystery of Christ and the Church', in Walter M. Abbott SJ (ed.), *The Documents of Vatican II,* Geoffrey Chapman, London, 1967.